Modelling with force and motion

The School Mathematics Project

CAMBRIDGE
UNIVERSITY PRESS

Main authors   Stan Dolan
                    Judith Galsworthy
                    Mike Hall
                    Janet Jagger
                    Ann Kitchen
                    Paul Roder
                    Tom Roper
                    Mike Savage
                    Bernard Taylor
                    Carole Tyler
                    Nigel Webb
                    Julian Williams
                    Phil Wood

Team leader   Ann Kitchen

Project director   Stan Dolan

Many others have helped with advice and criticism.

This unit has been produced in collaboration with the Mechanics in Action Project, based at the Universities of Leeds and Manchester.

The authors would like to give special thanks to Ann White for her help in producing the trial edition and in preparing this book for publication.

The publishers would like to thank the following for supplying photographs:

Front cover – Trustees of the Science Museum, London;
page 52 – Mechanics in Action Project;
page 53 – Mechanics in Action Project;
page 75 – NASA;
page 98 – Nicholas Judd.

Published by the Press Syndicate of the University of Cambridge
The Pitt Building, Trumpington Street, Cambridge CB2 1RP
40 West 20th Street, New York, NY 10011–4211, USA
10 Stamford Road, Oakleigh, Victoria 3166, Australia

© Cambridge University Press 1992

First published 1992

Produced by Gecko Limited, Bicester, Oxon.

Cover design by Iguana Creative Design

Cartoons by Tony Hall

Printed in Great Britain at the University Press, Cambridge

British Library cataloguing in publication data

A catalogue record for this book is available from the British Library.

ISBN 0 521 40891 1

Contents

1 Projectiles

1.1 Weight

In *Newton's laws of motion* you met the idea of a force. A force is simply a measure of the strength of a push or pull. For example, you already know that an apple of mass 0.1 kg is pulled to the Earth by a force of approximately 1 newton.

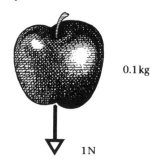

0.1 kg

1 N

The purpose of this unit is to examine further the connection between force and motion so that you can better understand complicated motion such as that illustrated below:

One of the remarkable features of Newton's mathematical model of mechanical motion is that you only need a knowledge of a very few different types of force to be able to model so much of the physical world. This section will reconsider the pulling force called **weight**. The next tasksheet looks at the historical development of ideas that led to the formulation of Newton's law of gravitation.

TASKSHEET 1 — Newton's law of gravitation (page 24)

Newton's law of gravitation

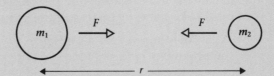

If two particles of masses m_1 and m_2 kg are at a distance r metres apart, they will attract each other with a force of magnitude

$$F = \frac{Gm_1 m_2}{r^2} \text{ newtons}$$

where G is a universal constant, called the constant of gravitation.

$$G = 6.673 \times 10^{-11} \text{ N m}^2\text{kg}^{-2}$$

The gravitational force per unit mass due to the Earth is g newtons per kilogram. It varies from place to place on the Earth's surface, having a value of 9.8321 at the poles and 9.7799 at the equator. This is often approximated to 9.8 or 10.

When you model the gravitational attraction of the Earth by a single 'downwards' force of mg newtons, you are making many assumptions.

In the picture above, the Earth's gravitational attraction on the skier has been modelled by a single force, a weight **W**.

Many assumptions have been made in formulating such a simple model. List as many of these assumptions as possible, together with your own comments as to how reasonable they seem. Can you think of some situations where these assumptions would not be appropriate?

E X A M P L E   1

Calculate the force of attraction between the Moon and an astronaut of mass 80 kg standing on its surface, using the following data:

mass of Moon = 7.34×10^{22} kg
approximate radius of Moon = 1738 km

How does this compare with the force of attraction due to the Earth that she would experience while standing on the Earth's surface?

S O L U T I O N

By Newton's law of gravitation, force $= \dfrac{80 \times 7.34 \times 10^{22} \times 6.67 \times 10^{-11}}{1\,738\,000 \times 1\,738\,000}$

$= 129.7\,\text{N}$

So the force of attraction is approximately 130 newtons.

The force of attraction she would experience on the Earth's surface is about 80 g newtons. This is roughly 800 newtons; six times greater than the force on the Moon.

E X E R C I S E   1

(Use G = 6.67×10^{-11} N m^2 kg^{-2} and g = 9.8 N kg^{-1})

1   Calculate the force of attraction between a shot of mass 1 kg and a telephone directory of mass 1.5 kg if they are 1 m apart on the floor. Why do they not pull together?

2   A 4 kg mass is allowed to fall from rest. What is its change in momentum after 3 seconds?

During the same time interval, the Earth experiences an equal but opposite change in momentum. Assuming that the Earth has a mass of 5.98×10^{24} kg, what is the effect on the Earth's velocity?

3 A 5 kg mass is allowed to fall from rest and after t seconds the velocity is $49 \, \text{m s}^{-1}$.
Calculate:

(a) the change in momentum;

(b) the length of time it has been falling;

(c) the distance through which it has fallen.

4 An unknown mass is allowed to fall from rest. In 4 seconds the change of momentum is $78.4 \, \text{kg m s}^{-1}$. Find the mass and its velocity after the 4 seconds.

5

Assume that the Earth is a perfect sphere of mass $5.974 \times 10^{24} \, \text{kg}$ and radius $6.378 \times 10^6 \, \text{m}$ and that the gravitational constant is 6.673×10^{-11}. Then the weight of a stone of mass 1 kg is calculated as 9.80 newtons at sea level.

(a) Calculate its weight

(i) at the top of the Eiffel Tower (322 m above sea level);

(ii) at the top of Mount Everest (8.848 km above sea level);

(iii) at the edge of the stratosphere (928 km above sea level).

(b) Calculate its weight in a space capsule orbiting the Earth in a circular orbit whose radius is twice the radius of the Earth.

(c) Sketch a graph of weight against distance above sea level for a 1 kg mass, using the values given above.

6 A mass of 3 kg is projected vertically upwards with a speed of $49 \, \text{m s}^{-1}$. At two instants in time, the speed of the mass is measured as $9.8 \, \text{m s}^{-1}$. How long after the mass was thrown upwards were the measurements made?

7E The forces acting on a descending parachutist of mass 70 kg are assumed to be his weight and a constant retarding force. His velocity is $24.5 \, \text{m s}^{-1}$ four seconds after starting from rest. Find the magnitude of the retarding force.

1.2 Motion under gravity

In *Newton's laws of motion* you looked at the motion of bodies which are free to fall under the influence of gravity. How does gravity affect the motion of bodies which are launched into the air?

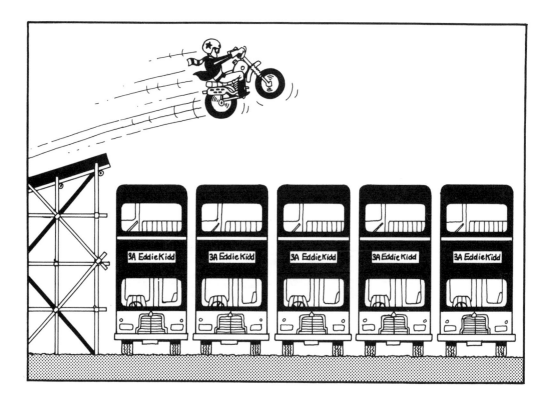

(a) Imagine that you are asked to design a stunt like the one illustrated above. Estimate how fast Eddie Kidd's bike should go to clear 20 buses.

(b) What can you say about its velocity on landing?

(c) What other mathematical questions might you ask which would help you plan the stunt successfully?

In the next tasksheet you will attempt to model Eddie Kidd's motion.

TASKSHEET 2 — *Jumping buses (page 27)*

1.3 **Velocity**

Eddie Kidd's position every fifth of a second has been marked on the graph given below.

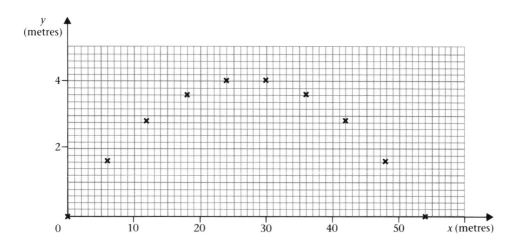

His position vectors at intervals of 0.2 seconds are given in the table below. (All distances are in metres.)

t	0.0	0.2	0.4	0.6	0.8	1.0	1.2	1.4	1.6	1.8
$\begin{bmatrix} x \\ y \end{bmatrix}$	$\begin{bmatrix} 0 \\ 0 \end{bmatrix}$	$\begin{bmatrix} 6 \\ 1.6 \end{bmatrix}$	$\begin{bmatrix} 12 \\ 2.8 \end{bmatrix}$	$\begin{bmatrix} 18 \\ 3.6 \end{bmatrix}$	$\begin{bmatrix} 24 \\ 4.0 \end{bmatrix}$	$\begin{bmatrix} 30 \\ 4.0 \end{bmatrix}$	$\begin{bmatrix} 36 \\ 3.6 \end{bmatrix}$	$\begin{bmatrix} 42 \\ 2.8 \end{bmatrix}$	$\begin{bmatrix} 48 \\ 1.6 \end{bmatrix}$	$\begin{bmatrix} 54 \\ 0 \end{bmatrix}$

To enable you to investigate the flight mathematically it is useful to first obtain a general expression for Eddie's position vector during the flight, t seconds after take-off.

Complete the formula for Eddie's position at time t.

$$\begin{bmatrix} x \\ y \end{bmatrix} = \begin{bmatrix} ? \\ 9t - 5t^2 \end{bmatrix}$$

Check that your formula fits the data given above.

If a particle is travelling in a straight line with constant velocity **v**, then:

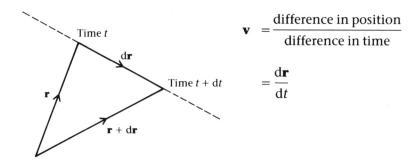

$$\mathbf{v} = \frac{\text{difference in position}}{\text{difference in time}}$$

$$= \frac{\mathrm{d}\mathbf{r}}{\mathrm{d}t}$$

Of course, Eddie is **not** travelling in a straight line. However, if you magnify a small section of his flight you will find that it is locally straight.

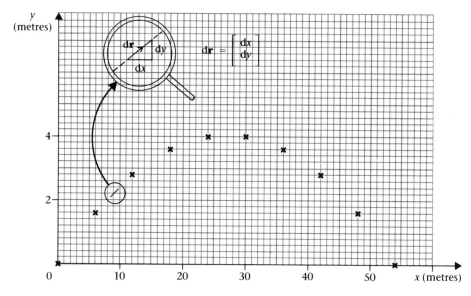

(a) Explain why $\mathbf{v} = \begin{bmatrix} \dfrac{\mathrm{d}x}{\mathrm{d}t} \\ \dfrac{\mathrm{d}y}{\mathrm{d}t} \end{bmatrix}$.

(b) Hence find **v** for $\mathbf{r} = \begin{bmatrix} 30t \\ 9t - 5t^2 \end{bmatrix}$.

(c) Calculate **v** when $t = 0.7$, 0.9 and 1.1 seconds.

(d) What is Eddie's speed when he lands?

(e) Interpret and validate your solutions.

The position vector **r** and velocity vector **v** of a projectile (or any other particle) are connected by:

$$\mathbf{v} = \frac{d\mathbf{r}}{dt}$$

$\dfrac{d\mathbf{r}}{dt}$ can be found by differentiating each component of **r**.

$$\frac{d\mathbf{r}}{dt} = \begin{bmatrix} \dfrac{dx}{dt} \\ \dfrac{dy}{dt} \end{bmatrix}$$

E X A M P L E   2

The position vector of a golf ball, t seconds after being hit, is given by

$$\begin{bmatrix} x \\ y \end{bmatrix} = \begin{bmatrix} 10t \\ 30t - 5t^2 \end{bmatrix}$$ (All distances are in metres.)

Find the golf ball's speed when it first strikes the ground (assumed to be horizontal).

S O L U T I O N

It strikes the ground when $30t - 5t^2 = 0$

$$5t(6 - t) = 0$$
$$\Rightarrow \quad t = 0 \text{ or } 6$$

Its velocity in $\mathrm{m\,s^{-1}}$ is given by $\mathbf{v} = \begin{bmatrix} 10 \\ 30 - 10t \end{bmatrix}$.

After 6 seconds, $\mathbf{v} = \begin{bmatrix} 10 \\ -30 \end{bmatrix}$ and its speed is $\sqrt{(10^2 + 30^2)} \approx 31.6\,\mathrm{m\,s^{-1}}$.

E X E R C I S E   2

1   For the golf ball in example 2, find

(a) the time at which its velocity is horizontal;

(b) its maximum height;

(c) the horizontal distance it travels before it hits the ground.

2 Using the data for Eddie Kidd given earlier in this section, what is Eddie's speed

(a) when he leaves the ramp;

(b) at the top of his flight?

3 Cannon-ball Kate is being fired out of a cannon into a safety net in a stunt to raise money for charity. Her position vector in metres is given by

$$\mathbf{r} = \begin{bmatrix} 10t \\ 9t - 5t^2 + 2 \end{bmatrix}$$

If the landing net is 2 metres square and is placed at a height of 2 metres above the ground,

(a) should her landing net be at $\begin{bmatrix} 18 \\ 2 \end{bmatrix}$ or $\begin{bmatrix} 20 \\ 2 \end{bmatrix}$;

(b) what is her speed when she lands in the net?

4 A shot has position vector $\mathbf{r}$ metres at time t seconds given by

$$\mathbf{r} = \begin{bmatrix} 10t \\ 2 + 10t - 5t^2 \end{bmatrix}$$

Calculate

(a) the magnitude and direction of the velocity of projection;

(b) the acceleration;

(c) the height above ground level at which it was released by the shot-putter;

(d) the distance of the throw;

(e) the velocity of the shot on striking the ground;

(f) when the velocity of the shot is horizontal;

(g) the maximum height it attains above the ground.

5 The centre of gravity of a long-jumper, at time t seconds, has position vector

$$\mathbf{r} = \begin{bmatrix} 0.5 + 10t \\ 0.75 + 2.8t - 5t^2 \end{bmatrix} \text{ metres}$$

where the origin is taken to be the take-off board.

(a) What is the initial or take-off velocity of the long-jumper?

(b) Where is her centre of gravity on take-off?

(c) Assume that on landing the centre of gravity is at the same height as on take-off. For how long is the jumper in the air and how long is the jump?

1.4 Acceleration under a constant force

The velocity of a projectile changes throughout the motion. In *Newton's laws of motion* you obtained the following result for the flight of a golf ball:

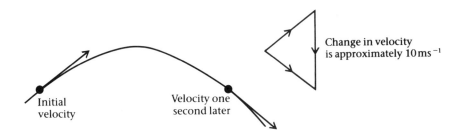

Change in velocity is approximately $10\,\text{ms}^{-1}$

Initial velocity

Velocity one second later

(a) Explain how the result above can be expressed as

$$\frac{\mathrm{d}\mathbf{v}}{\mathrm{d}t} = \begin{bmatrix} 0 \\ -10 \end{bmatrix}.$$

(b) Check this result for Eddie Kidd's motion, starting from

$$\mathbf{r} = \begin{bmatrix} 30t \\ 9t - 5t^2 \end{bmatrix}.$$

The vector $\dfrac{\mathrm{d}\mathbf{v}}{\mathrm{d}t}$ is called the **acceleration** of the projectile.

You should note that the acceleration is a vector in the same direction (vertically downwards) as the only force acting on the projectile – its weight. This can be obtained directly from Newton's second law:

force × time = change in momentum

(a) From the equation

force × time = change in momentum

explain how to obtain the alternative form of Newton's second law:

force = mass × acceleration

(b) Hence explain the connection between the acceleration of a projectile and g (the gravitational force per unit mass).

For any motion

  force = mass × acceleration

where acceleration is the rate of change of velocity.

For a projectile, the acceleration due to gravity is

approximately $\begin{bmatrix} 0 \\ -10 \end{bmatrix} \mathrm{m\,s^{-2}}$.

It is important to note that $\mathbf{F} = m\mathbf{a}$ is a vector equation, so acceleration is a vector quantity and the acceleration vector and the force vector must act in the same direction. Any object will therefore accelerate in the direction of the resultant force acting upon it. This is true even if the force is not constant.

EXAMPLE 3

A 3 kg stone slides across the surface of a frozen lake in such a way that its position vector $\mathbf{r}$ metres at time t seconds is given by

$$\mathbf{r} = \begin{bmatrix} t^2 - 20t + 80 \\ -2t^2 + 40t \end{bmatrix} \qquad 0 \le t \le 10$$

Find the force acting on the stone. Show that this force is constant and acts in the opposite direction to the velocity of the stone.

SOLUTION

By differentiating,

$$\mathbf{v} = \begin{bmatrix} 2t - 20 \\ -4t + 40 \end{bmatrix} \qquad \mathbf{a} = \begin{bmatrix} 2 \\ -4 \end{bmatrix}$$

From Newton's second law, $\mathbf{F} = m\mathbf{a} = 3\begin{bmatrix} 2 \\ -4 \end{bmatrix} = 6\begin{bmatrix} 1 \\ -2 \end{bmatrix}$,

therefore the force is $\begin{bmatrix} 6 \\ -12 \end{bmatrix} = 6\begin{bmatrix} 1 \\ -2 \end{bmatrix}$ newtons.

The force is constant and parallel to the vector $\begin{bmatrix} 1 \\ -2 \end{bmatrix}$.

For $0 \le t \le 10$, $\mathbf{v} = (20 - 2t)\begin{bmatrix} -1 \\ 2 \end{bmatrix}$ is in the direction of the

vector $\begin{bmatrix} -1 \\ 2 \end{bmatrix}$. Hence $\mathbf{F}$ acts in the opposite direction to the motion of the stone and is presumably due to friction or air resistance.

EXERCISE 3

1 A ball is thrown so that it has position vector $\mathbf{r} = \begin{bmatrix} 5t \\ 6t - 5t^2 + 1 \end{bmatrix}$ metres.

Calculate the velocity and acceleration of the ball.

2 An ice hockey puck is hit so that it has position vector

$\mathbf{r} = \begin{bmatrix} 9t - t^2 \\ 9t - t^2 + 1 \end{bmatrix}$ metres for $0 \leqslant t \leqslant 4.5$ seconds.

If the puck has mass 100 grams, find the force acting on the puck.

3 A skater's position on the ice is given by the position vector

$\mathbf{r} = \begin{bmatrix} 5t - t^2 \\ 3 + 5t - t^2 \end{bmatrix}$ metres for $0 \leqslant t \leqslant 2.5$ seconds.

Calculate the velocity and acceleration of the skater.
If the skater weighs 70 kg, calculate the force acting on him.

4 A child pulls a toy car along by means of a string, exerting a constant force on the string. If the position vector of the car, $\mathbf{r}$ metres at time t seconds, is

given by $\mathbf{r} = \begin{bmatrix} 3t^2 \\ 4t^2 \end{bmatrix}$ and its mass is 500 grams, calculate the magnitude

and direction of the pull exerted by the child.

5E In each of the following cases a particle is moving in such a way that its position vector is $\mathbf{r}$ metres at time t seconds. In each case:

- sketch the course on which the particle moves between $t = 0$ and $t = 4$;

- find its acceleration;

- find its acceleration at $t = 2$ and sketch its vector representation on your curve.

(a) $\mathbf{r} = \begin{bmatrix} t \\ t^2 \end{bmatrix}$ (b) $\mathbf{r} = \begin{bmatrix} 4t \\ 4t^{-1} \end{bmatrix}$

(c) $\mathbf{r} = \begin{bmatrix} \cos t \\ \sin t \end{bmatrix}$ (d) $\mathbf{r} = \begin{bmatrix} t \\ 3t \end{bmatrix}$

1.5 Projectile motion

The motion of bodies which are thrown, dropped or launched into the air under the influence of gravity is called **projectile motion**. You can study this motion using vector equations for position, velocity or acceleration.

For any projectile motion, the only force acting is taken to be weight, $\mathbf{W} = m\mathbf{g}$, acting downwards.

Taking axes horizontally and vertically upwards, $\mathbf{W} = \begin{bmatrix} 0 \\ -mg \end{bmatrix}$

Hence Newton's second law, $\mathbf{F} = m\mathbf{a}$, gives $\mathbf{a} = \begin{bmatrix} 0 \\ -g \end{bmatrix}$

In order to find out more about the velocity and position vector of a projectile, you will need to set up a model and analyse it.

TASKSHEET 3 — Projectile motion (page 28)

$\mathbf{a} = \dfrac{d\mathbf{v}}{dt}$, so integrating acceleration gives velocity.

$\mathbf{v} = \dfrac{d\mathbf{r}}{dt}$, so integrating velocity gives displacement.

The initial conditions of motion give the constants of integration.

EXAMPLE 4

A girl puts a shot with velocity $\begin{bmatrix} 2 \\ 3.5 \end{bmatrix} \mathrm{m\,s^{-1}}$. If she releases it 1.5 metres above the ground, show that it hits the ground after 1 second. Find its speed of impact.

SOLUTION

Assume that the shot is a particle of mass m kg and that air resistance can be neglected. Let the point of release be O and the point where it hits the ground be A.

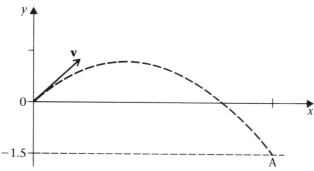

Take axes as shown.

Let $g = 10\,\text{m}\,\text{s}^{-2}$ downwards.

The force acting is $\begin{bmatrix} 0 \\ -mg \end{bmatrix}$ so the acceleration is $\dfrac{d\mathbf{v}}{dt} = \begin{bmatrix} 0 \\ -10 \end{bmatrix}$

By integration, $\mathbf{v} = \begin{bmatrix} 0 + c_1 \\ -10t + c_2 \end{bmatrix}$

When $t = 0$, $\quad \mathbf{v} = \begin{bmatrix} 2 \\ 3.5 \end{bmatrix} \Rightarrow \mathbf{v} = \begin{bmatrix} 2 \\ 3.5 - 10t \end{bmatrix}$

Thus $\dfrac{d\mathbf{r}}{dt} = \begin{bmatrix} 2 \\ 3.5 - 10t \end{bmatrix} \Rightarrow \mathbf{r} = \begin{bmatrix} 2t + d_1 \\ 3.5t - 5t^2 + d_2 \end{bmatrix}$

When $t = 0$, $\quad \mathbf{r} = \begin{bmatrix} 0 \\ 0 \end{bmatrix} \Rightarrow \mathbf{r} = \begin{bmatrix} 2t \\ 3.5t - 5t^2 \end{bmatrix}$

When $t = 1$, $\quad \mathbf{r} = \begin{bmatrix} 2 \\ -1.5 \end{bmatrix}$.

The shot hits the ground 2 metres away after 1 second.

When $t = 1$, $\quad \mathbf{v} = \begin{bmatrix} 2 \\ -6.5 \end{bmatrix}$.

The speed of impact is $\sqrt{(4 + 42.25)} = 6.8\,\text{m}\,\text{s}^{-1}$.

EXERCISE 4

In this exercise, ignore the effects of air resistance and take g to be $10\,\text{m}\,\text{s}^{-2}$.

1 Ann throws a ball to Julian with initial velocity $\begin{bmatrix} 7 \\ 5 \end{bmatrix}\,\text{m}\,\text{s}^{-1}$ and Julian

catches it at the same height. For how long was the ball in the air? How far apart were Ann and Julian?

2 A high-jumper takes off with initial velocity $\begin{bmatrix} 3 \\ 5 \end{bmatrix}\,\text{m}\,\text{s}^{-1}$.

At take-off her centre of gravity is approximately 1 metre above the ground. Write down the velocity and position vector of her centre of gravity at time t seconds after take-off.

What is the maximum height of her centre of gravity?

3 A discus is projected at an angle of $40°$ with a speed of $21\,\text{m s}^{-1}$ and from a height above the ground of 2 metres.

Calculate its velocity and position vector at time t. What is the length of the throw?

4E

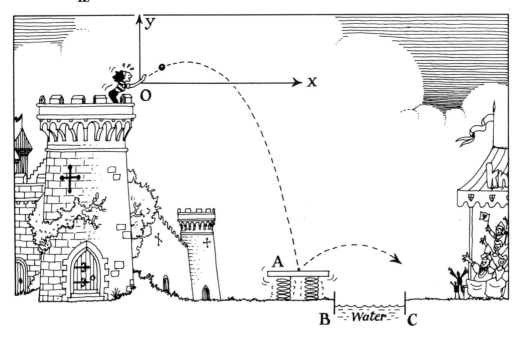

The picture shows a contestant in a TV game show standing on top of a tower. She hurls a cannon-ball of mass 8 kg from point O. Her objective is to make the cannon-ball bounce on a smooth horizontal platform at A, and then rebound across the water hazard BC. Taking axes through O as shown and with units of metres, A is the point $(8, -10)$ and C is $(11, -12)$.

(a) If the initial velocity is $\begin{bmatrix} 4 \\ 5 \end{bmatrix}\text{m s}^{-1}$ show that the cannon-ball

will land at A when two seconds have elapsed, with velocity

$\begin{bmatrix} 4 \\ -15 \end{bmatrix}\text{m s}^{-1}$.

(b) Assuming that momentum is conserved in the collision between the cannon-ball and the sprung platform (which can be modelled as a heavy, smooth rigid block of mass 48 kg, and which acquires a velocity

$\begin{bmatrix} 0 \\ -3 \end{bmatrix}\text{m s}^{-1}$ immediately after impact), show that the initial

velocity of the cannon-ball as it bounces off the block is $\begin{bmatrix} 4 \\ 3 \end{bmatrix}\text{m s}^{-1}$.

(c) Does the cannon-ball clear the water hazard?

1.6 The general case

For a more general case of projectile motion, you could take axes to be horizontal (x) and vertical (y) such that, at $t = 0$, the projectile has position vector $\begin{bmatrix} a \\ b \end{bmatrix}$ and initial velocity $\begin{bmatrix} u_x \\ u_y \end{bmatrix}$.

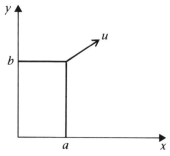

Assume that the only force acting is gravity.

So $\mathbf{a} = \dfrac{d\mathbf{v}}{dt} = \begin{bmatrix} 0 \\ -g \end{bmatrix}$

(a) Find by integration a vector equation giving the velocity $\mathbf{v}$ at time t.

(b) By integrating again show that the position vector $\mathbf{r}$ is given by

$$\mathbf{r} = \begin{bmatrix} u_x t + a \\ -\tfrac{1}{2} g t^2 + u_y t + b \end{bmatrix}$$

Usually, projectile motion assumes projection from the origin with velocity of magnitude u at an angle ϕ to the horizontal.

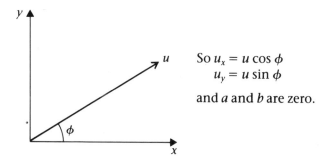

So $u_x = u \cos \phi$
$u_y = u \sin \phi$

and a and b are zero.

This gives $\mathbf{v} = \begin{bmatrix} u \cos \phi \\ -gt + u \sin \phi \end{bmatrix}$ and $\mathbf{r} = \begin{bmatrix} ut \cos \phi \\ -\tfrac{1}{2} g t^2 + ut \sin \phi \end{bmatrix}$

(a) When $t = \dfrac{2u \sin \phi}{g}$, calculate **r**.

(b) Interpret your result. How can it be validated?

(c) At the highest point on the path of a projectile, the vertical component of the velocity is zero. Use this fact to find an expression, in terms of u, g and ϕ, for the time taken to reach the highest point.

(d) Use this result to show that the height reached is $\dfrac{u^2 \sin^2 \phi}{2g}$.

(e) Interpret this result as u and ϕ vary. Validate it practically.

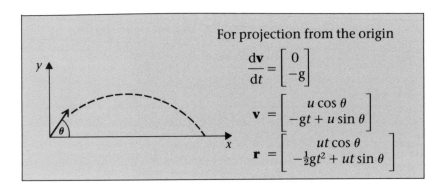

For projection from the origin

$$\frac{d\mathbf{v}}{dt} = \begin{bmatrix} 0 \\ -g \end{bmatrix}$$

$$\mathbf{v} = \begin{bmatrix} u \cos \theta \\ -gt + u \sin \theta \end{bmatrix}$$

$$\mathbf{r} = \begin{bmatrix} ut \cos \theta \\ -\tfrac{1}{2}gt^2 + ut \sin \theta \end{bmatrix}$$

EXERCISE 5

(Take g as $10 \, \mathrm{m \, s^{-2}}$ and ignore air resistance.)

1 At a given instant, a group of objects is projected horizontally from the edge of a table. Each object has a different initial speed.

What can you say about the motion of each object as time increases?

2 A golf ball is hit so that it leaves the ground with initial velocity of magnitude $25 \, \mathrm{m \, s^{-1}}$, at an angle α, where $\tan \alpha = \tfrac{4}{3}$, as shown in the diagram.

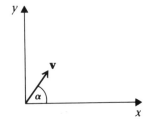

(a) How high does the ball go?

(b) How far does it travel before its first bounce if the ground is horizontal?

3   Two children throw stones into the sea. Jill throws her stone at an angle of 60° to the horizontal and speed $20\,\mathrm{m\,s^{-1}}$, while Jack throws his stone at a 40° angle and can only manage an initial speed of $15\,\mathrm{m\,s^{-1}}$. Both stones are thrown simultaneously and both are released at a height 1.4 m above sea level.

    (a) How high does Jill throw her stone?

    (b) Which stone lands in the water first?

    (c) Whose stone lands furthest away?

4   A small relief plane is flying horizontally at $30\,\mathrm{m\,s^{-1}}$. Its height is 210 m. A package is released from the plane and just clears some trees which are 30 m high.

    (a) At what horizontal distance from the trees is the package released?

    (b) How far beyond the trees does the package land?

5   Ahmed throws a ball to Susan who is 80 m away and who catches it at the same height as it was thrown. The ball is in the air for 5 seconds. Taking the acceleration g as $9.8\,\mathrm{m\,s^{-2}}$, find the initial velocity of the ball.

6   At what angle should a projectile be launched if it is to achieve the maximum possible horizontal range?

Find out the greatest recorded distance a cricket ball has ever been thrown. Estimate the initial speed of the ball.

7   A rugby player takes a penalty kick. He places the ball at a point O on the ground, 12 metres away from the goal line and directly in front of the goal, and he kicks it at a right angle to the goal line at an angle of 40° to the horizontal. The ball passes over the crossbar at point P, 4 metres above the ground. Estimate the initial speed of the ball.

1.7 Modelling with projectiles

 All the situations pictured above could be modelled as projectile motion.

(a) What assumptions should you make in each case? How valid are your assumptions?

(b) What other situations can you think of which might be modelled using projectile motion?

Once the model has been set up, the problem can be analysed using vector equations for projectile motion.

You may wish to use one of the ideas in the discussion point as a basis for your extended investigation. This is discussed further in chapter 5.

> What mathematical questions might you ask about juggling?

A wide range of questions arise from most of the situations given. Try to use practical experiments where appropriate to validate your analysis and interpretation.

After working through this chapter you should:

1 know that Newton's law of gravitation states that

$$F = \frac{Gm_1m_2}{r^2}$$ where G is a universal constant called the constant of gravitation;

2 know that the acceleration of a body is its rate of change of velocity

$$\mathbf{a} = \frac{d\mathbf{v}}{dt}$$

(acceleration is a vector and has both magnitude and direction);

3 know that Newton's second law can be stated as

$$\mathbf{F} = m\mathbf{a}$$

(the force and acceleration must act in the same direction);

4 know that in projectile motion, the only force is assumed to be weight, acting vertically downwards;

5 know how to model projectile motion in a variety of problems and situations.

Newton's law of gravitation

Throughout history, astronomers have studied the motion of the planets. The Greeks assumed that the universe was geocentric, i.e. they assumed that the Earth was at the centre. In Alexandria, Claudius Ptolemy used this geocentric model to predict the motions of the planets, often with great accuracy. In fact the geocentric model remained dominant until 1543, when Copernicus claimed that the Sun, and not the Earth, was the centre about which the planets moved.

Later, in 1609, Johannes Kepler challenged the circular motion assumption. From observational data, Kepler realised that the paths of the planets were not perfect circles. He asserted that they move in elliptical orbits about the Sun.

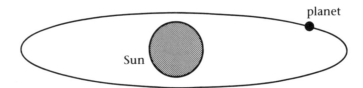

It became clear that the basic assumptions of the geocentric model were false. It was replaced by a heliocentric model in which the Sun is the centre of our solar system about which the planets move in elliptical orbits.

Isaac Newton was born in 1642 and went to Cambridge to study natural science. An important problem at that time was to explain the force that kept the planets rotating about the Sun, and the Moon rotating about the Earth.

When you swing a conker round on the end of a string, the pull of the string keeps the conker rotating about your hand. Similarly, there has to be a force acting on the Moon causing it to rotate about the Earth.

Newton realised that the force which keeps the Moon spinning round the Earth is the same as that which causes objects to fall to the ground. He called it the **force due to gravity**, and in 1667 he proposed a law of gravitation.

Newton's law of gravitation

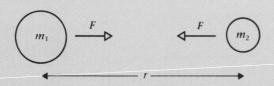

If two particles of mass m_1 kg and m_2 kg are at a distance r metres apart, they will attract each other with a force of magnitude

$$F = \frac{Gm_1m_2}{r^2} \text{ newtons}$$

where G is a universal constant, called the constant of gravitation.

The value of the universal constant can be determined by a method introduced by Henry Cavendish in 1798. He set up an experiment where two small lead spheres each of mass 0.75 kg were hung from the ends of a 2 metre wooden rod. The centre of the rod was suspended by a long fine wire. When two heavy lead spheres, each of mass 250 kg, were placed near the two small spheres the attraction between the large and small spheres caused the rod to turn. By measuring the twist in the wire he calculated the force of attraction and hence the constant G. He placed the experiment in a draught-free room and viewed the end of the rod from the garden, using a telescope.

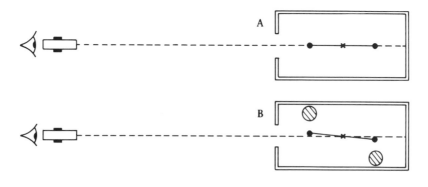

The work of Cavendish showed that G = 0.000 000 000 066 N m² kg⁻², within 1% of its modern value of 6.673×10^{-11}. This provided a direct verification of Newton's law of gravitation which had previously only been tested using astronomical data.

The consequences of Newton's law are enormous. It says that any two bodies will attract each other whether they are two planetary bodies like the Moon and the Earth, or two bodies on the Earth like the book and ball shown below.

The gravitational force on an object due to the Earth is called its weight.

The force of attraction between an object on the Earth's surface and the Earth itself is given by the equation

$$F = G\,\frac{mE}{r^2}$$

where m is the mass of the object, E is the mass of the Earth and r is the radius of the Earth.

The radius r had been known to the ancient Greeks; it is approximately 6.4×10^6 metres. Furthermore, $\dfrac{F}{m}$ is easy to measure simply from observations of a falling object. The mass of the Earth, however, could not be calculated until Cavendish had obtained his results.

1 What is meant by '$\dfrac{F}{m}$ is easy to measure'? What is an approximate value for $\dfrac{F}{m}$?

2 Use Cavendish's value for G to determine the mass of the Earth.

Jumping buses

Find a model for the motion of Eddie Kidd.

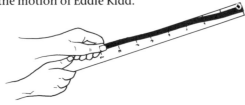

Hints:
Use a small, thin stretchy rubber band and a ruler to simulate the bike and rider.
Hook the rubber band on the ruler. Pull it back and then release it.
Take care where you aim it.
Use the same rubber band each time.

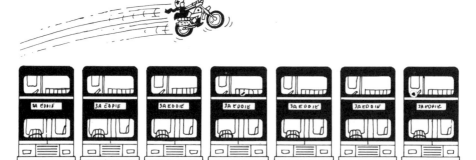

1   Place a target about 2 metres away. Aim your band from the same level, so that it lands on the target consistently. What angle are you firing at? Mark your ruler so you know how far to stretch the band for your given angle of projection.

2   Fire your band vertically upward using the same setting. How high does it travel?

3   Use this measurement, h, to calculate your speed of projection, u. Remember that v changes by $9.8 \, \mathrm{m \, s^{-1}}$ each second.

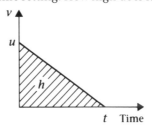

4   Using the same speed, u, alter your angle of projection. What do you notice about:

   (a) the range;

   (b) the maximum height;

   (c) the time in the air?

Projectile motion

$\boxed{\text{Problem}}$ To find the highest point, the landing point and the flight time for an elastic band fired at a speed of $4.4\,\mathrm{m\,s^{-1}}$ at an angle of $30°$.

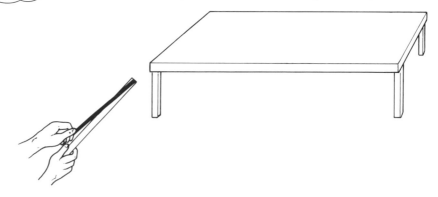

$\boxed{\begin{array}{c}\text{Set up a}\\ \text{model}\end{array}}$ Assume the elastic band is a particle, projected from point A with a speed of $4.4\,\mathrm{m\,s^{-1}}$ at $30°$ to the horizontal table AB. The elastic band then flies for t seconds and lands R metres along the table at B.

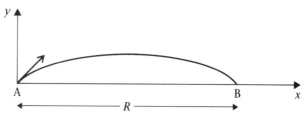

Choose x and y axes as shown, so that A has coordinates $(0, 0)$ and B has coordinates $(R, 0)$. Assume that the elastic band of mass m has constant weight mg, where $g = 9.8\,\mathrm{m\,s^{-2}}$. What other assumptions are made in this model?

$\boxed{\begin{array}{c}\text{Analyse}\\ \text{the problem}\end{array}}$ The problem is to calculate R and t.

The acceleration is $\mathbf{a} = \begin{bmatrix} 0 \\ -g \end{bmatrix} = \begin{bmatrix} 0 \\ -9.8 \end{bmatrix}\mathrm{m\,s^{-2}}$

You need to find the velocity $\mathbf{v}$ after any time t. Remember that if you can differentiate $\mathbf{v}$ to obtain $\mathbf{a}$, you can integrate $\mathbf{a}$ to obtain $\mathbf{v}$.

$$\frac{d\mathbf{v}}{dt} = \begin{bmatrix} 0 \\ -9.8 \end{bmatrix}$$

Integrating, $\mathbf{v} = \begin{bmatrix} C_1 \\ -9.8t + C_2 \end{bmatrix}$ where C_1 and C_2 are constants.

The initial velocity is $4.4\,\mathrm{m\,s^{-1}}$ at an angle of 30° and so

$$\mathbf{v} = \begin{bmatrix} 4.4\cos 30° \\ 4.4\sin 30° \end{bmatrix} = \begin{bmatrix} 3.81 \\ 2.2 \end{bmatrix} \text{ where } t = 0$$

Therefore $\begin{bmatrix} C_1 \\ C_2 \end{bmatrix} = \begin{bmatrix} 3.81 \\ 2.2 \end{bmatrix}$ and $\mathbf{v} = \begin{bmatrix} 3.81 \\ 2.2 - 9.8t \end{bmatrix}$

The horizontal component of velocity is a constant $3.81\,\mathrm{m\,s^{-1}}$, but the vertical component is decreasing at $9.8\,\mathrm{m\,s^{-2}}$.

The band is at its highest point when $\mathbf{v} = \begin{bmatrix} 3.81 \\ 0 \end{bmatrix}\mathrm{m\,s^{-1}}$

i.e. when $0 = 2.2 - 9.8t \Rightarrow t = 0.224$ seconds

1   Integrate $\mathbf{v}$ to find the position vector $\mathbf{r}$ of the elastic band at time t.

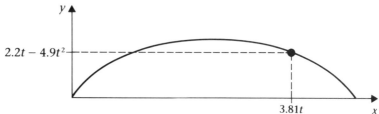

At the band's highest point $t = 0.224$ seconds, $y = 2.2t - 4.9t^2$ and so $y = 0.247$ metres.

Now consider the time, t, taken to land at B, where the y-coordinate is zero.

$$2.2t - 4.9t^2 = 0$$

2   (a) Solve the equation $2.2t - 4.9t^2 = 0$ to find t.

   (b) Use this value to find the range.

Interpret /validate

3   What are your conclusions?

4   Validate your results experimentally. What difficulties and errors arise?

2 Forces

2.1 Contact forces

In *Newton's laws of motion* you saw that:

> Unless acted upon by an external force, a particle travels with
> constant velocity.
> The resultant force on an object is equal to its rate of change of
> momentum (its change in momentum each second).
> When two bodies interact, they exert equal but opposite forces
> upon each other.

One type of pushing force with which you will be very familiar is
that of a contact force between surfaces.

If a box rests on a table then the box pushes against the table and the
table pushes against the box. **R** is the total contact force on the box
from the table. In this case, Newton's third law says that there is an
equal but opposite force acting on the table.

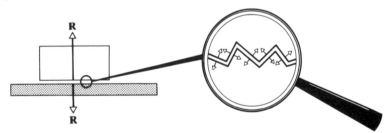

You can model the situation with a large number of 'contact forces'.
Note that the sum of all the contact forces on the box gives the total
contact force. This is conventionally modelled as a single force.

The most useful force diagram to draw is usually one showing **all**
the forces acting on one object. For a box on a table you might draw:

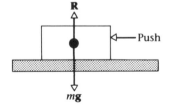

There is no acceleration vertically
and so by Newton's first law

$$\mathbf{R} - m\mathbf{g} = 0$$
$$\text{or} \qquad \mathbf{R} = m\mathbf{g}$$

Even when the box is on a slope, if it does not move then the contact force is vertically upwards to maintain the equilibrium and again **R** = mg. Note that **R** is not perpendicular to the surface.

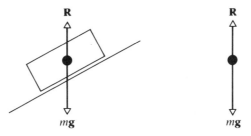

Objects are modelled as particles. This is done by drawing a dot in the object and showing **all** the forces acting on the dot, as shown above.

It is sometimes convenient to consider the contact force as a combination of two forces, a **normal contact force** perpendicular to the surface and a force called **friction** which acts parallel to the surfaces in such a direction as to oppose any tendency to slide.

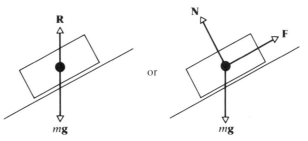

or

N and **F** are called components of the contact force **R**. This idea is studied further in a later section. It is important to note that you can use either **R** or its components but **not both** on the same diagram.

If a box is pushed across a rough horizontal surface, friction opposes the motion and the force diagram is:

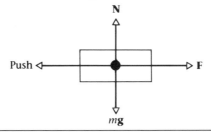

(a) What can be said about the four forces on the box if it does not move?

(b) Draw a force diagram for the box above, replacing **N** and **F** by a single contact force **R**.

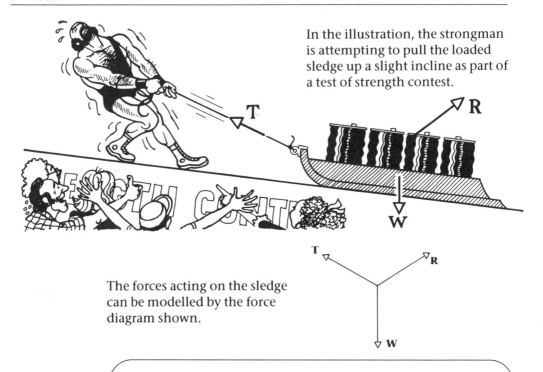

In the illustration, the strongman is attempting to pull the loaded sledge up a slight incline as part of a test of strength contest.

The forces acting on the sledge can be modelled by the force diagram shown.

Describe each of the forces represented above. Draw another version of the force diagram replacing **R** by a normal contact force and a friction force.

The contact force, **R**, of one object on another may be replaced by a normal contact force, **N**, perpendicular to the surface, and a friction force, **F**, parallel to the surface which acts to oppose motion. This friction force may, of course, be zero.

EXERCISE 1

1 The six diagrams provide models of the forces acting on various objects. For each, give a possible description of the forces.

(a)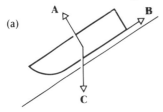

A sledge sliding down a slope

(b)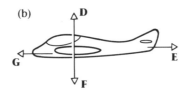

An aeroplane in flight

(c)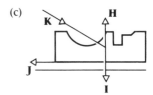

A toy being pushed across a floor by a child leaning over it (d)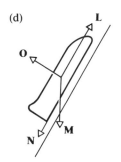

(e)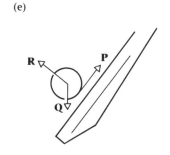

(f)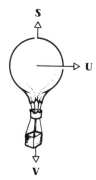

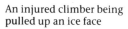

An injured climber being
pulled up an ice face

A ball being
struck with a bat

A hot-air balloon ascending and
being blown by a side wind

2 Draw a force diagram for the injured climber of question 1 (d) if she is being winched **down** the cliff face.

3 Draw a force diagram for a toy being pulled across the floor by a string:

    (a) if the contact force between the floor and the toy is shown as a single force;

    (b) if the contact force is divided into its two components.

4 For each of the following situations draw a diagram to model the forces you think are appropriate. Consider the object in bold type.

    (a) a **girl** sliding on a toboggan

    (b) the **toboggan** in part (a)

    (c) a **car** being given a push start by a man

    (d) the **man** in part (c)

    (e) a **ship** at anchor

    (f) a **ski-jumper** when she is in the air

    (g) a **parachutist** in mid-air falling straight down

2.2 Adding forces

The picture shows two girls using ropes to hold a heavy object just above the ground.

Describe what happens to the pull from the ropes if the girls are standing:

(a) close together;

(b) one metre apart;

(c) four metres apart.

Try this practically using a heavy schoolbag and some string. Can you lift the bag high enough so that the strings are horizontal? Explain your answer.

In *Newton's laws of motion* you learnt that forces are vectors. This implies that they can be added in just the same way as displacement and velocity.

The combined effect of a number of forces is known as the **resultant** force. The resultant of two forces can be found by adding the forces as vectors. This can be done by drawing either a triangle of forces or a parallelogram of forces.

If **R** is the resultant of **P** and **Q**, then **R** = **P** + **Q**.

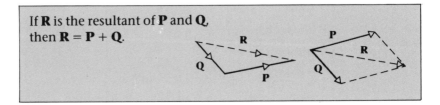

Find the resultant of the two forces 5 newtons and 7 newtons which contain an angle of 70°.

S O L U T I O N

Draw a parallelogram ABCD with AD = 5 units and AB = 7 units and angle BAD = 70°

Measure AC and angle ϕ

AC = 9.9 units and angle ϕ = 28°

Hence the resultant is a force of 9.9 newtons at an angle of 28° to the 7 newton force.

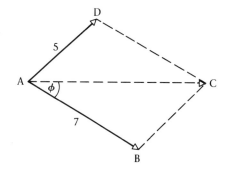

How can you find the resultant of three or more forces?

If a body is either at rest or moving with constant velocity, its acceleration is zero. The vector sum of the forces acting on the body is zero and hence the forces form a closed polygon.

E X A M P L E   2

The three forces shown acting on a particle are in equilibrium. Find the magnitude and direction of **P**.

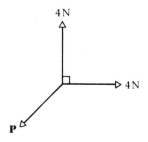

S O L U T I O N

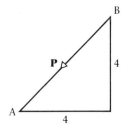

The forces are in equilibrium so their resultant is zero. Their vectors form a closed polygon.

P is therefore represented in magnitude and direction by $\overrightarrow{BA}$.

So **P** has magnitude 4 √2 newtons and acts in a direction of 135° with each 4N force.

The following experiments will enable you to investigate these ideas practically. Each group should report back to the class, giving a clear description of their experiment and the conclusions they have reached.

TASKSHEET 1 — Investigating forces (page 52)

EXERCISE 2

1   Find the resultants of the pairs of forces shown in the diagrams.

(a)   (b)

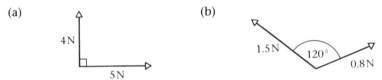

2   Gillian and Paul are shown giving Zia's car a push start.

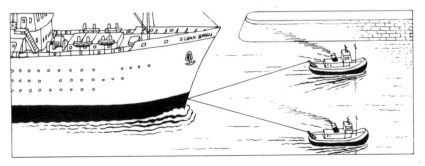

Gillian pushes straight ahead with a force of 420N. Paul pushes with a force of 500N at an angle of 25° to the line of the car. Use a scale drawing to find both the magnitude and the direction of the resultant of these two pushes.

3   Two tugs are towing a large ship into harbour, pulling on the bows of the ship with horizontal cables. The far tug is pulling with a force of 52000N at an angle of 23° to the forward motion of the ship and the near tug pulls with a force of 68000N at an angle of 18° to the motion. Use a scale drawing to find the resultant pull on the ship.

4   The frictional force between an object and the ground is 80N. If the normal contact force is 200N then calculate the magnitude and direction of the total contact force.

5   Two forces of magnitude 3N and 4N have a resultant of magnitude 6N. Find, by scale drawing, the angle between the two forces.

6   The following groups of forces are in equilibrium. Find the magnitude and direction of the labelled forces:

(a)   (b)

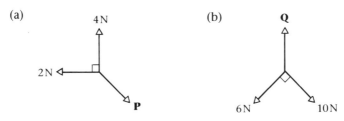

(c)   (d)

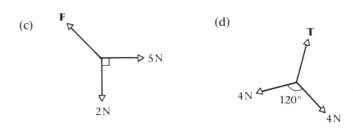

7   A shopping bag of mass 15kg is carried by two people. If they walk so that their arms make an angle of 50° with the horizontal, what force must each of them exert on the bag? Estimate the likely minimum angle at which they can hold the bag.

2.3 Resolving forces

In section 2.1, a total contact force **R** was considered as the sum of a frictional force **F** and a normal contact force **N**.

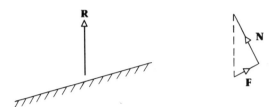

Splitting a force into components at right angles to each other is easy to do using simple trigonometry.

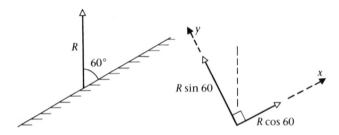

The use of components can be helpful in solving problems because the components in a particular direction can be added very easily.

E X A M P L E   3

Calculate the answer to question 3 of exercise 2.

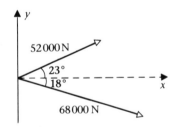

S O L U T I O N

$$\mathbf{R} = \begin{bmatrix} 52\,000\cos 23° \\ 52\,000\sin 23° \end{bmatrix} + \begin{bmatrix} 68\,000\cos 18° \\ -68\,000\sin 18° \end{bmatrix} = \begin{bmatrix} 112\,538 \\ -695 \end{bmatrix}$$

$R^2 = 112\,538^2 + 695^2 \qquad R = 112\,540$

$$\tan\phi = \frac{-695}{112\,538} \Rightarrow \phi = -0.4° \text{ (to 1 d.p.)}$$

The resultant pull is 113 000 N (to 3 s.f.) at an angle of 0.4° (to the nearest 0.1°) to the line of motion of the ship.

In general any force **F** can be resolved into two perpendicular components $F \cos \phi$ and $F \sin \phi$ acting in the directions shown.

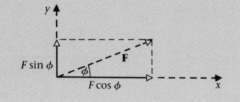

$$\mathbf{F} = \begin{bmatrix} F \cos \phi \\ F \sin \phi \end{bmatrix}$$

EXERCISE 3

1 The force **F** is of magnitude 50 newtons at 30° to the horizontal. In each of the following cases resolve **F** into its components

(a) horizontally and vertically;

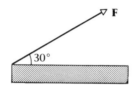

(b) up the slope and perpendicular to the slope;

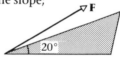

(c) down the slope and perpendicular to the slope.

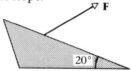

2 Resolve the following forces into perpendicular components in the directions indicated:

(a)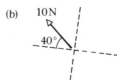

(b)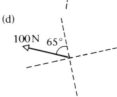

(c)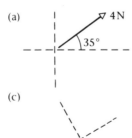

(d)

39

3

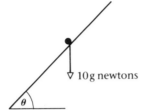

A mass of 10kg is resting on a rough inclined plane as shown.

(a) Draw a force diagram and, by considering components parallel to the plane, calculate the magnitude of the force of friction, F, if $\theta = 20°$.

(b) If N is the magnitude of the normal contact force, show that

$$\frac{F}{N} = \tan \theta$$

4 By resolving one or both forces into components, calculate the resultant of the forces 11N and 9N shown in the diagram.

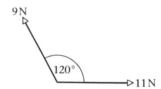

5 By resolving each force into components, find the resultant of the following sets of forces.

(a)

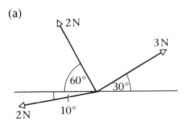

(b)

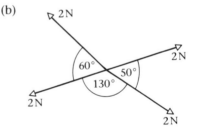

6 Three children each think that a parcel has stopped at them in a game of 'pass the parcel'. They pull on parts of the parcel with forces of 20N, 40N and 35N at angles of 120°, 150° and 90° with each other as shown in the diagram.

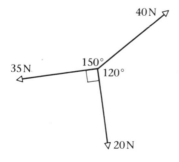

If the parcel does not break, in which direction will it move?

7 The diagram shows a scout held (at rest) by two ropes. The mass of the scout is 60 kg. Find the tension in each of the ropes

(a) by taking components horizontally and vertically;

(b) by taking components parallel and perpendicular to one of the ropes.

8 Two masses of *m* grams each are suspended over two friction-free pulleys. A mass of 60 grams is hung between them as shown. If the strings both make an angle of 45° to the vertical, find *m*.

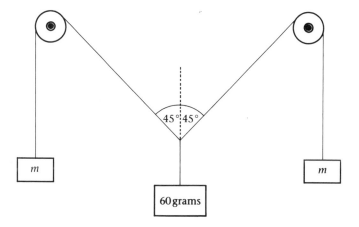

9 A mass of 20 kg is supported by two inelastic strings inclined to the vertical at 30° and 60°. Calculate the tension in each string.

2.4 Force and acceleration

In section 2.1 the following diagram was obtained when modelling the sledge being pulled up the slope.

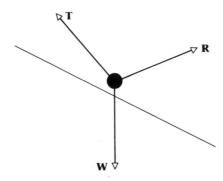

The values for some of the angles and forces have been included on the diagram below. The total contact force is split into a normal contact force and a friction force of 250N.

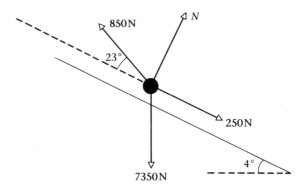

What does the weight of 7350 newtons tell you about the mass of the sledge?

Finding N is quite easy if you make a good choice of directions in which to resolve the forces. What directions would you choose?

Find N and also find the resultant force on the sledge.

What is the acceleration of the sledge?

The choice of directions in which to resolve the forces can be critical for finding straightforward solutions to problems.

E X A M P L E   4

A book of mass 3 kg is placed on a smooth slope of angle 25°. It starts to slide down the slope. What is the contact force on the book? What is its acceleration?   (Take g = 10 N kg^{-1}.)

S O L U T I O N

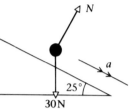

The slope is smooth so the contact force is normal to the slope. The acceleration is a m s^{-2} down the slope. Taking axes along and perpendicular to the slope,

$$\text{by Newton's second law} \begin{bmatrix} 30 \sin 25° \\ N - 30 \cos 25° \end{bmatrix} = 3 \begin{bmatrix} a \\ 0 \end{bmatrix}$$

$$30 \sin 25° = 3a \Rightarrow a = 4.23$$

$$\text{and } N - 30 \cos 25° = 0 \Rightarrow N = 27.2$$

The contact force is 27.2 newtons at right angles to the slope (to 3 s.f.). The book accelerates down the slope at 4.23 m s^{-2} (to 3 s.f.).

E X E R C I S E   4

(Take g = 10 N kg^{-1}.)

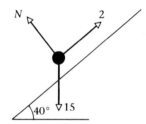

1   A block is sliding down a slope. The forces acting on it are shown in the diagram (in newtons). Find the normal contact force N newtons. What is the acceleration of the block?

2   A trolley of mass 200 kg is being pulled up a smooth slope of 20° by a rope parallel to the slope. If the tension in the rope is 800 newtons, find the acceleration of the trolley.

3   A girl of mass 65 kg is abseiling down a rope fixed to the top of a cliff. If the tension in the rope is 540 newtons, what is the resultant force on the girl? Find her acceleration. What happens if the rope breaks?

4   A ball of mass 1 kg is falling through the air with an acceleration of 6 m s^{-2}. Calculate the air resistance.

5   A woman weighing 90 kg is standing in a lift. What is the magnitude of the contact force between her and the lift if the lift is moving

(a) upwards with constant speed;   (b) upwards with acceleration 1.5 m s^{-2};
(c) downwards with acceleration 1.5 m s^{-2}?

2.5 Models of static friction

A man is trying to push a heavy crate across a warehouse floor.
It is too hard to move so more and more people come to help.
It finally moves when there are 5 people pushing.
Discuss the friction force between the crate and the floor.
Is it constant the whole time?
What might it depend on?
Set up a class experiment,
as shown, to find out how
static friction, F newtons,
depends on the normal
contact force, N newtons.

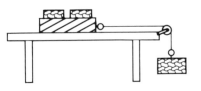

Data from friction experiments often give a variety of linear and
non-linear models for **limiting friction**. The limiting friction may
vary dramatically from point to point on a surface of contact. The
models below were fitted to experimental data collected by some
students.

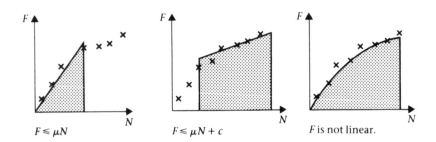

$F \leqslant \mu N$ $F \leqslant \mu N + c$ F is not linear.

Are the models valid for the same range of N? Why is the
inequality sign used?

For static friction, the model usually used is $F \leqslant \mu N$.

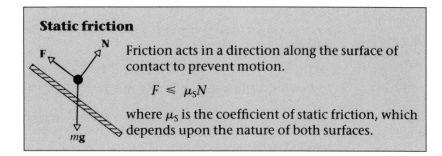

Static friction

Friction acts in a direction along the surface of contact to prevent motion.

$$F \leqslant \mu_S N$$

where μ_S is the coefficient of static friction, which depends upon the nature of both surfaces.

Typical values and ranges of values of μ_S are:

Surfaces in contact	μ_S
wood against wood	0.2–0.5
wood against metal	0.2–0.6
metal against metal	0.15–0.3
plastic against rubber	0.7
sandpaper against sandpaper	2.0
metal on snow	0.02

E X A M P L E   5

A box is placed on a rough plane which is gradually tilted. The box is on the point of sliding when the plane makes an angle of α to the horizontal. Find the coefficient of static friction between the box and the plane.

S O L U T I O N

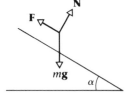

Let the friction force be **F** newtons and the normal contact force be **N** newtons, as shown. The forces are in equilibrium. Using Newton's second law:

$$\mathbf{F} + \mathbf{N} + m\mathbf{g} = 0$$

$$\begin{bmatrix} F \\ 0 \end{bmatrix} + \begin{bmatrix} 0 \\ N \end{bmatrix} + \begin{bmatrix} -mg \sin \alpha \\ -mg \cos \alpha \end{bmatrix} = 0$$

$$\Rightarrow F = mg \sin \alpha \quad \text{and} \quad N = mg \cos \alpha$$

But $F = \mu N$ as the box is about to slide

so $mg \sin \alpha = \mu \, mg \cos \alpha$

$$\Rightarrow \mu = \tan \alpha$$

EXERCISE 5

[Take $F \leqslant \mu_S N$ for your model of static friction and g $= 10\,\mathrm{m\,s^{-2}}$.]

1 A crate of weight 100 newtons rests on a rough plane inclined at 30° to the horizontal. It is just about to slip.

(a) What is the force due to friction on the crate?

(b) Find the coefficient of static friction between the crate and the plane.

2 A rubber of mass m kilograms is placed on a table. The coefficient of static friction between the two surfaces is 0.7. What is the greatest angle at which the table can be tilted before the rubber starts to slide?

3 A climber of mass 65 kg is practising traversing a slab of rock. The coefficient of friction between her feet and the rock is 1.2.

(a) What is the greatest angle of slope she can walk on?

(b) What is the force due to friction at that point?

4 A sledge of mass 150 kg is being held on a snowy slope by a rope parallel to the slope. If the slope makes an angle of 35° to the horizontal and the coefficient of static friction is 0.02, what is the least force required

(a) to hold it stationary;

(b) to start it moving up the slope?

5 A climber of mass 100 kg is being held stationary on a rough slope of angle 80° to the horizontal by his partner at the top of the slope.

If the coefficient of static friction between the climber and the slope is 0.9 what are the limits on the tension in the rope?

2.6 Models of sliding friction

When you solve problems you generally need to make assumptions about the forces which act. In particular, you need to have reasonable 'models' for friction, tension and air resistance in various situations. A 'reasonable model' for a force involves making assumptions about the force which experience tells you have worked well in similar situations. Scientists and engineers have collected a number of 'standard models' of this kind which are now in common use, though it is **impossible to guarantee** that they will work in any new situation and they are usually only **approximately** true. In the last section you looked at some models for static friction. In this section you will consider friction when objects are sliding.

> What assumptions could you make about the magnitude and direction of the friction force in each of the situations above?

The tasksheet looks at **sliding friction** to see how different models, or assumptions, can be used.

TASKSHEET 2 — Curling (page 54)

47

Sliding friction

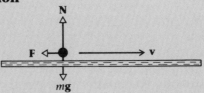

The friction force always acts in the direction opposed to the velocity of the body relative to the surface of contact.

(a) $F = 0$ if the object is moving on a smooth surface (e.g. a puck on ice for a short period of time).

(b) $F = \mu_D N$ where μ_D is the coefficient of sliding friction and N is the normal contact force.

μ_D is normally less than μ_S for any two bodies in contact.

EXAMPLE 6

A box of mass 20 kg is being pushed across a rough floor at constant velocity by a horizontal force of 20 newtons. Using the model for sliding friction $F = \mu N$, what is the coefficient of sliding friction μ?

What force must be used if the mass of the box is doubled?

SOLUTION

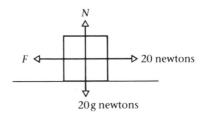

Let the friction be F newtons and the normal contact force be N newtons.
The box does not accelerate vertically or horizontally, so by Newton's second law
$N = 200$ and $F = 20$
Then $F = \mu N$
$\Rightarrow \mu = 0.1$

If the mass of the box is doubled, N is doubled and $F = 0.1 \times 400$
$$= 40$$

The push must be 40 newtons horizontally.

EXERCISE 6

1   A block of mass 6 kg will move at constant velocity when pushed along a table by a horizontal force of 24 N. Find the coefficient of friction between the block and the table.

2   A puck of mass 0.1 kg is sliding in a straight line on an ice rink. The coefficient of sliding friction between the puck and the ice is 0.02. Find the resistive force due to friction and then find the speed of the puck after 20 seconds if its initial speed is $10 \, \mathrm{m \, s^{-1}}$.

3   A particle of mass 1 kg is projected at $5 \, \mathrm{m \, s^{-1}}$ along a rough horizontal surface. The coefficient of sliding friction is 0.3. Assuming that $F = \mu N$, how far does the particle move before coming to rest?

4   A gymnast of mass 80 kg is sliding down a vertical climbing rope with constant speed. The coefficient of friction between his hands and the rope is 0.3. Calculate the total normal contact between his hands and the rope. State any assumptions you make.

5E   A particle rests on a rough plane inclined at an angle ϕ to the horizontal.

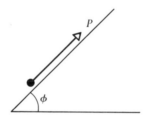

When an additional force P is applied as shown, the particle slides down the slope at constant speed.

Show that $P = mg (\sin \phi - \mu \cos \phi)$ where m is the mass of the particle and μ is the coefficient of friction.

If the additional force is trebled to $3P$, and the particle now moves up the plane with constant speed, show that

$$\tan \phi = 2\mu$$

2.7 Modelling forces

In sections 2.5 and 2.6 you looked at different friction forces and their models. Some models are simpler to use than others and you should always start with the simplest appropriate model. Tension and air resistance can also be modelled.

TASKSHEET 3 — Modelling with force (page 57)

All the situations in the picture could be modelled using contact forces.

What assumptions should you make in each case?

How valid are your assumptions?

What other situations could be modelled using contact forces?

Many of the ideas in this chapter could provide the basis of an extended investigation.

After working through this chapter you should:

1   be able to find the resultant of several forces on a particle;

2   be able to use this resultant to find the acceleration of the particle;

3   know that if a particle is in equilibrium then the resultant force acting on it is zero; a particle that is in equilibrium will either remain at rest or travel with constant velocity;

4   be able to resolve a force, $\mathbf{F}$, into two components, $F \sin \phi$ and $F \cos \phi$;

5   be able to model situations involving friction, tension and resistance.

Investigating forces

The students shown in the photographs are doing experiments to validate the following statements.

1 The resultant of two forces can be found by adding the forces as vectors, using a triangle of forces (or parallelogram of forces).

2 If a particle is in equilibrium then the vector sum of the forces acting on it is zero.

3 Three or more forces can be added by drawing a vector polygon.

Working in groups, carry out your own experiments to validate one or more of the above. You may want to use some of the ideas shown or design your own experiment. You should report your findings to the rest of the class afterwards.

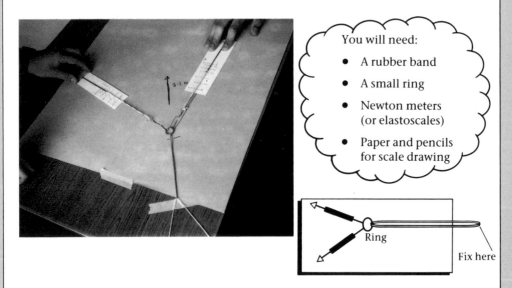

You will need:

- A rubber band
- A small ring
- Newton meters (or elastoscales)
- Paper and pencils for scale drawing

Ring

Fix here

Hints:
- Loop one end of the rubber band round the ring and fix the other end to the table.
- Hook a couple of newton meters in the ring and use them to stretch the rubber band to a certain length.
- Draw line vectors on the paper to model, in magnitude and direction, the pulls of the newton meters on the ring.
- Now use a single newton meter to extend the rubber band to the same point.
- Draw a line vector representing the pull of the single newton meter on the ring.

What can you say about the three force vectors you have drawn?

You will need:

- Two pulleys
- Three sets of masses
- String
- Paper and pencils for scale drawing

Hints:

- Tie three pieces of string together in a knot at A and put loops in the other ends of the strings.

- Suspend the masses on the pulleys in front of a sheet of paper as shown.

- Draw line vectors on the paper to model the forces acting on the knot at A.

What can you say about the three force vectors you have drawn?

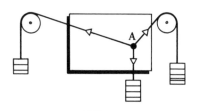

You will need:

- String
- Newton meters (or elastoscales)
- Paper and pencils for scale drawing

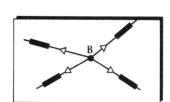

Hints:

- Tie four pieces of string together in a knot B. Put loops in their other ends.

- Hook a newton meter in each loop and pull them tight on a sheet of paper.

- Draw line vectors on the paper to model, in magnitude and direction, the pull of each of the newton meters on the knot B.

What can you say about the four force vectors you have drawn?

Curling

Problem

What model of friction would be appropriate for a curling stone travelling along the ice?

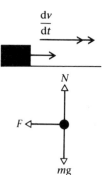

The data below was collected for a curling stone from the moment it left the curler's hand until it came to rest.

Displacement x (metres)	0	5	10	15	20	25	30	35	40
Time t (seconds)	0	2.5	5.5	8.5	11.9	16.2	21.7	31.1	–

Set up a model

Assume that the stone is a particle of mass m kg and that air resistance can be ignored. Let the friction force be F and the velocity be $v\,\mathrm{m\,s^{-1}}$.

The key assumption concerns the friction F. First, try the model $F = 0$.

Model 1: Sliding friction is zero

Analyse the problem

Apply Newton's second law

$$\begin{bmatrix} -F \\ N - mg \end{bmatrix} = m \begin{bmatrix} \dfrac{dv}{dt} \\ 0 \end{bmatrix}$$

$F = 0$ and so $\dfrac{dv}{dt} = 0$

Therefore v is a constant, u, say.
Then $x = ut$

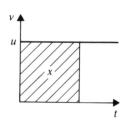

<table>
<tr><td>

Interpret
/validate

</td><td>

The stone continues to slide
at speed u for ever.
In fact this result is a reasonable
model for the first 20 metres of
the motion:

</td></tr>
</table>

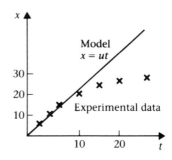

1 Find a value for u which best fits the first 20 metres of the motion.

You can see that the model does
not fit the data well for values of t
greater than 10 seconds.

It is clear that the graph of (t, x)
should be a curve.

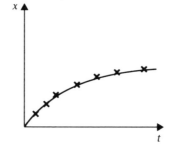

2 What conclusion should you reach about the model $F = 0$

(a) for the first few seconds of the motion;

(b) for the motion when $t > 10$ seconds?

You can now refine the model for the second part of the motion.

<table>
<tr><td>

Set up a
model

</td><td>

The only assumption you need to change is $F = 0$.
Now let F be constant throughout the motion.

</td></tr>
</table>

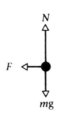

Model 2: Sliding friction is constant during the motion

| Analyse the problem |

Applying Newton's second law

$$\begin{bmatrix} -F \\ N - mg \\ 0 \end{bmatrix} = m \begin{bmatrix} \dfrac{dv}{dt} \\ \\ \end{bmatrix}$$

Therefore $-F = m \dfrac{dv}{dt}$ and $N - mg = 0$

$$\dfrac{dv}{dt} = \dfrac{-F}{m}$$

Integrating gives $v = u - \dfrac{Ft}{m}$ and $x = ut - \dfrac{Ft^2}{2m}$

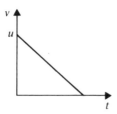

| Interpret /validate |

The stone comes to rest after $t = \dfrac{um}{F}$ seconds.

The faster it is projected, the longer it takes to stop. It is clear that after this point the model becomes invalid.

You must now match the equation

$$x = ut - \dfrac{F}{2m} t^2$$

against the data collected previously.

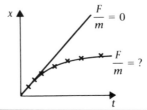

3 (a) What value of $\dfrac{F}{m}$ will give a reasonable fit for this set of data?

(b) What can you conclude about the model F = constant for a stone sliding until it comes to rest?

Modelling with force

Choose one of the situations below.

Select a suitable standard model or models for the analysis from the lists of standard models at the end of the tasksheet. Test your solution using the apparatus suggested.

Prepare a report for the rest of the class.

1   How does the tension in a spring or elastic string vary with its extension?

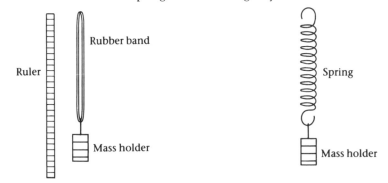

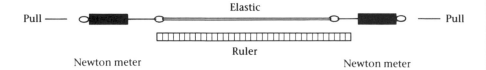

2   What effect does the surface area of a balloon have on the resistance acting on it? Drop 4 identical balloons from a height 2 metres and measure the time they take to reach the ground.

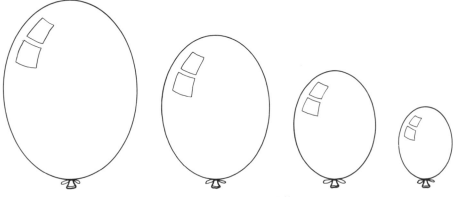

4 identical balloons blown up to different sizes

Standard models for resistance to motion through a medium such as air or water

1 Negligible resistance

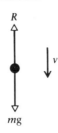

The resistive force is small compared to the other forces acting parallel to it and it may be ignored.

$$R = 0$$

2 R = constant

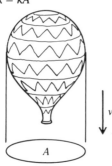

If the variation in resistance is small compared to the other forces acting, for example, when a parachute is open and the parachute descends at nearly zero acceleration, then the resistance can be taken as constant and the body is said to travel at terminal velocity.

Other models which may be used are:

3 $R = kv$

In normal motion, the resistive force is proportional to the velocity of the object through the resistive medium.

4 $R = kv^2$

For motion at high speeds, the resistive force can be taken to be proportional to the square of the velocity of the object through the resistive medium.

5 $R = kA$

The resistive force at any velocity can be taken to be proportional to the area normal to the direction of motion relative to the resistive medium.

Standard models for tension

The simplest model for tension is that of a light inextensible string.

1 A light string or chain   If a string has negligible mass then the tension at one end of the string is assumed to be the same as that at the other end of the string even if the ends are pulled apart in a vertical line.

$$T_1 = T_2$$

2 An inextensible string or chain   If a string is 'inextensible' you can assume that it does not stretch. The tension T can take any value up to a breaking value T_B.

$$0 \leqslant T \leqslant T_B$$

Other models which may be appropriate are:

3 A heavy string or chain   If a heavy string or chain of mass m is hung vertically from one end then the tension in the string varies such that

$$T_1 = T_2 + mg$$

4 A light elastic spring or string   If a string or spring can stretch under tension then the tension can be assumed to vary with the extension. Hooke's model states that, for a given range of extension x, $T = kx$ where k is the spring stiffness and depends on the length of the spring or string and the material it is made from. The tension has a fixed limit beyond which the string will break.

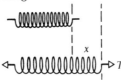

5 A pretensioned elastic string or spring   Some springs or strings require an initial tension before they will start to stretch. They then obey Hooke's model up to a breaking point.

$$T \leqslant T_0 \text{ for } x = 0$$

$$T = T_0 + kx \text{ for } 0 < x \leqslant x_0$$

3 Acceleration and circular motion

3.1 The motion of the Moon

This chapter will consider acceleration which is not constant. Acceleration is a vector and can therefore change its magnitude or its direction or both.

The direction of the acceleration of a body is always in the direction of the resultant force acting. This may not be in the direction of motion, as can be seen clearly by considering the motion of the Moon.

What force is acting on the Moon?
What does this tell you about the direction of its acceleration?
In what direction is the Moon travelling?
Is its velocity changing? What about its acceleration?

EXERCISE 1

(Use $G = 6.67 \times 10^{-11} \, \text{N} \, \text{m}^2 \, \text{kg}^{-2}$.)

1 (a) Calculate the magnitude of the force due to the Earth acting on the Moon, using the following data:

mass of Moon = $7.34 \times 10^{22} \, \text{kg}$
mass of Earth = $5.98 \times 10^{24} \, \text{kg}$
average radius of the Moon's orbit = 3.8×10^8 metres

(b) Use Newton's second law to deduce the magnitude and direction of the Moon's acceleration.

2 (a) Calculate the force of attraction of the Sun on the Earth using Newton's law of gravitation and hence deduce the magnitude and direction of the acceleration of the Earth due to the pull of the Sun.

The mass of the Sun is $2.0 \times 10^{30} \, \text{kg}$, that of the Earth is $5.98 \times 10^{24} \, \text{kg}$ and the average distance between their centres is $1.50 \times 10^8 \, \text{km}$.

(b) The maximum distance between the centres of the Sun and the Earth is $1.52 \times 10^8 \, \text{km}$ and the minimum distance is $1.47 \times 10^8 \, \text{km}$. Find the range of the force of attraction between the Sun and the Earth.

3 The first orbiting laboratory, Skylab, was set in orbit at an altitude of 434 km on 14 May 1973. Crews were ferried to and from the laboratory by means of Apollo-type spacecraft. With the Apollo command service module (CSM) attached, Skylab had an overall length of 36 m and a mass of 90 600 kg.

Calculate the force of attraction of the Earth on Skylab.

3.2 Angular speed and velocity

The motion of the Moon can be modelled by that of a penny stuck onto a rotating turntable.

TASKSHEET 1 — Investigating angular speed (page 72)

If the penny is 0.1 m from the centre of rotation and it rotates at $2 \, \text{rad s}^{-1}$, then the position of the penny at any time t is defined by the vector **r**, measured in metres, where

$$\mathbf{r} = \begin{bmatrix} 0.1 \cos 2t \\ 0.1 \sin 2t \end{bmatrix}$$

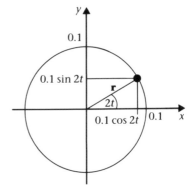

Being able to express precisely the position of the penny, for any value of t during the time it rotates, enables you to investigate its motion mathematically.

The velocity of the penny $\mathbf{v} = \dfrac{d\mathbf{r}}{dt}$ where **v** is measured in m s^{-1}.

So if $\mathbf{r} = \begin{bmatrix} 0.1 \cos 2t \\ 0.1 \sin 2t \end{bmatrix}$, then differentiating **r** gives $\mathbf{v} = \begin{bmatrix} -0.2 \sin 2t \\ 0.2 \cos 2t \end{bmatrix}$

(a) Calculate the position vector **r** and the velocity vector **v** for time t where $t = 0.5, 1, 1.5, 2, 2.5$ and 3 seconds.

(b) On a sheet of graph paper, draw a circle (reduced scale) to represent the penny on the turntable and mark the position and velocity vectors calculated above.

What can you say about the magnitude and direction of the velocity vector?

What can you say about the acceleration, $\dfrac{d\mathbf{v}}{dt}$, of the penny?

> If a particle is rotating with a constant angular speed of ω rad s^{-1} at a distance r from the centre, then in 1 second the particle travels a distance $r\omega$. The speed of the particle is given by $v = r\omega$.

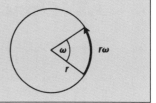

EXAMPLE 1

A grinding wheel of radius 5 cm is rotating at 6 r.p.m. What is its angular speed in rad s^{-1} and what is the speed of the edge of the wheel?

SOLUTION

6 r.p.m. $= 6 \times 2\pi$ or 37.7 radians per minute

i.e. $\dfrac{37.7}{60} = 0.628$ rad s^{-1} (to 3 s.f.)

The radius of the wheel is 5 cm, so in one second the edge of the wheel has moved a distance 5×0.628 cm. The speed is 3.14 cm s^{-1} (to 3 s.f.).

EXERCISE 2

1 A helicopter's rotor blade is 4 metres long and is rotating at 50 r.p.m. Find the speed of the blade tip.

2 An outboard motor is started by pulling a cord wound round a grooved wheel of radius 10 cm. If the cord is pulled at 1 m s^{-1} what is the angular speed of the wheel in rad s^{-1}?

3 The drum of a washing machine can rotate at between 500 and 1000 r.p.m. What are these in rad s^{-1}? If the diameter of the drum is 1.2 metres what is the range of speeds of points on the drum?

4 The Earth has radius 6.37×10^6 metres. It spins about its axis approximately once every 24 hours. What is the approximate speed of an object due to this rotation   (a) on the Earth's equator;   (b) at the north pole?

5 (a) The hand of a dial is rotating with angular speed 3 rad s^{-1}. What is the time for one revolution?

  (b) If its angular speed is ω rad s^{-1} and the time for one revolution is T seconds, find an equation linking T and ω.

6E The cotton from a cotton reel of radius 2 cm is pulled out with a constant speed of 3 m s^{-1}. What is the angular speed of the reel in rad s^{-1}? If the radius of an empty reel is 1 cm and the reel takes 50 minutes to empty, sketch a rough graph of angular speed against time. Give reasons for your sketch.

3.3 Circular motion

In section 3.1 you saw that the Moon travelled round the Earth in an approximately circular orbit due to a force acting towards the Earth. When any particle moves uniformly in a circle, it is straightforward to show that its acceleration is always directed towards the centre.

Consider a particle P moving about O in a circle radius r with uniform speed.

Moving uniformly means that the angle ϕ changes at a constant rate.

Thus $\phi = \omega t$ where ω is the angular speed, measured in $\text{rad}\,\text{s}^{-1}$.

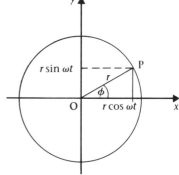

The displacement $\mathbf{r} = \begin{bmatrix} r\cos\omega t \\ r\sin\omega t \end{bmatrix}$

(a) Find the velocity by differentiation and show that its magnitude is constant. What is its direction?

(b) Show that the acceleration can be written as

$$\mathbf{a} = r\omega^2 \begin{bmatrix} -\cos\omega t \\ -\sin\omega t \end{bmatrix} \text{ or } \mathbf{a} = -\omega^2\mathbf{r}$$

What is its direction?

Show that its magnitude is $a = r\omega^2 = \dfrac{v^2}{r}$.

EXAMPLE 2

An astronaut is orbiting the Earth at a steady speed in a space capsule. The capsule is, on average, 12 800 km from the Earth's centre.

What is the time taken to complete an orbit?
What if the orbit radius were larger?

Set up a
model

Assume the space capsule is a particle and its weight, $\mathbf{F}$, is the only force acting. Let its mass by m kg. Assume the mass of the Earth is 5.98×10^{24} kg and $G = 6.67 \times 10^{-11}\,\text{N}\,\text{m}^2\,\text{kg}^{-2}$. Assume the orbit is a circle of radius 12 800 km.

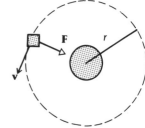

Analyse the problem

Working in SI units and using Newton's law

of gravitation, $F = \dfrac{GMm}{r^2}$

$$F = \frac{6.67 \times 10^{-11} \times 5.98 \times 10^{24} \times m}{(1.28 \times 10^7)^2}$$

$$= 2.43 \, m \, \text{newtons}$$

Using Newton's second law radially, $F = ma$ so $a = 2.43 \, \text{m s}^{-2}$
But $a = r\omega^2$ so $2.43 = 1.28 \times 10^7 \, \omega^2$
$\Rightarrow \omega = 4.36 \times 10^{-4} \, \text{rad s}^{-1}$

But $\omega = \dfrac{2\pi}{T}$ where T is the time for one orbit

$\Rightarrow T = 14\,400$ seconds (to 3 s.f.)

Interpret /validate

The space capsule orbits the Earth once every four hours.

If the orbit radius is r then $F = \dfrac{GMm}{r^2}$ and $F = mr\omega^2$

Therefore $\dfrac{GM}{r^2} = r\omega^2 \Rightarrow \omega^2 = \dfrac{GM}{r^3}$

So ω^2 is proportional to $\dfrac{1}{r^3}$

Since $T = \dfrac{2\pi}{\omega}$, T^2 varies as $\dfrac{1}{\omega^2}$.

T^2 is therefore proportional to r^3.
So for a satellite, the greater the orbit radius, the greater the time taken for an orbit. Equally, the greater the radius, the smaller the angular velocity.

> When seen on television an astronaut seems to float effortlessly round the capsule. Does this mean that the astronaut is weightless?

If a particle rotates with constant angular speed $\omega \, \text{rad s}^{-1}$ at a distance r metres from the centre of rotation then the speed of the particle is given by $r\omega \, \text{m s}^{-1}$ and the acceleration is $r\omega^2 \, \text{m s}^{-2}$ towards the centre of the circle.

$$v = r\omega \quad \text{and} \quad a = r\omega^2 = \frac{v^2}{r}$$

TASKSHEET 2 — Satellites (page 74)

EXERCISE 3

1   (a) Calculate the angular speed of the Moon about the Earth. (One
         revolution takes 27.32 days.)

    (b) Use the result $a = r\omega^2$ to calculate the acceleration of the Moon. (The
         radius of the Moon's orbit $= 3.8 \times 10^8$ metres.)

    (c) Compare your answer with the acceleration you calculated in exercise 1,
         question 1.

2   A racing car is travelling at a constant speed of $120\,\mathrm{km\,h^{-1}}$ round a bend
    consisting of part of a circle. The magnitude of its acceleration is $30\,\mathrm{m\,s^{-2}}$.
    What is the radius of the bend?

3   A roundabout in a children's playground is rotating at 10 revolutions a
    minute. The radius of the roundabout is 2 metres. A child of mass 30 kg sits
    on the seat. What are her speed and acceleration if she sits

    (a) 1 metre from the centre;

    (b) 2 metres from the centre?

    Describe how the force acting on the child alters as she changes her position
    on the roundabout.

4   A coin of mass 4 grams is placed on a turntable and rotates with constant
    angular speed $0.5\,\mathrm{rad\,s^{-1}}$. Write down its acceleration in metres per second^2
    when it is placed 15 cm from the axis of rotation. Calculate the magnitude
    of the resultant force on the coin. What can you deduce about the
    coefficient of friction between the turntable and the coin?

5   The coefficient of static friction between a block of wood and a turntable
    surface has been found to be 0.3. The block is placed 20 cm from the axis of
    rotation and the speed of the turntable is gradually increased. How fast is it
    rotating when the block slides off?

6E A group of ten skaters have linked arms to form the rotating diameter of a
    circle.

    (a) If they make one complete revolution every 6 seconds, describe the
         probable speeds of the various members of the group.

    (b) What is the acceleration of the outside pair?

    (c) Estimate the force needed to produce such an acceleration.

3.4 Acceleration

The diagram below shows the figure-of-eight track for a model car. A car is travelling round it at constant speed.

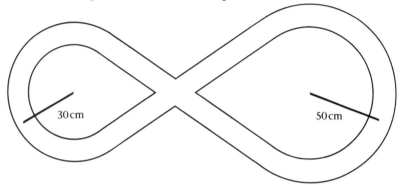

The car described above completes a lap of the track at a speed of $2\,\text{m}\,\text{s}^{-1}$.

(a) How does its velocity change as it goes round the track?

(b) How does its acceleration change? Calculate the maximum and minimum acceleration.

The velocity and acceleration can be shown conveniently on a diagram of the path of the model car by representing them by arrows, in the appropriate directions, of length proportional to the magnitudes involved. For instance, using a scale of $1\,\text{cm} : 1\,\text{m}\,\text{s}^{-1}$ and $1\,\text{cm} : 10\,\text{m}\,\text{s}^{-2}$, you can draw a diagram to show velocities and accelerations in three positions, P, Q and R below.

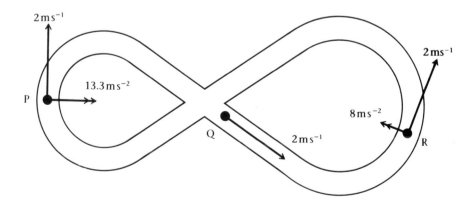

How have the magnitudes of the accelerations at P and R been calculated? Why is no acceleration shown at Q?

Many people think of acceleration as rate of change of speed, a scalar quantity. In mechanics the correct use of the term is as rate of change of velocity. Remember that it is a vector and has both magnitude and direction. The direction is always in the direction of the resultant force.

EXERCISE 4

1 An ice-skater moves with constant speed $20\,\mathrm{m\,s^{-1}}$ round a circle of radius $6\,\mathrm{m}$.

(a) Calculate his acceleration and show on a diagram the directions of his velocity and acceleration at two separate points on the circle.

(b) The speed is constant, but is the velocity constant? Justify your answer.

(c) Explain why the acceleration is not constant.

2 The drum of a small centrifuge spins at a constant $100\,\mathrm{r.p.m.}$ about a vertical axis. If the inside of the drum is $27\,\mathrm{cm}$ across, show that the acceleration of an object of mass 200 grams pressed against the wall of the drum is approximately $15\,\mathrm{m\,s^{-2}}$. What are the magnitude and direction of the resultant force required to produce this acceleration?

3

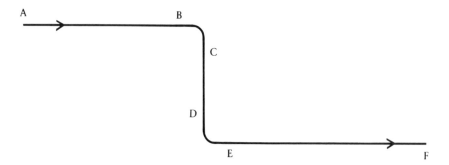

The diagram illustrates the shape of part of the layout for a model railway. The bends at BC and DE are circular, the other sections being straight. The train increases speed between A and B, travels with constant speed from B to E and then slows down from E to F.

(a) Mark on a diagram the direction of the acceleration between A and B, B and C, C and D, D and E, and E and F.

(b) How does the acceleration differ from the rate of change of speed at these various points?

4   At the points A, B, C and D draw vectors representing the acceleration of a
car moving around the track at a constant speed of $20\,\mathrm{m\,s^{-1}}$.

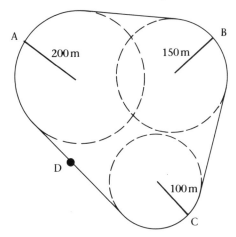

5E   A particle moves round a circle of radius 10 metres such that its angular
speed is not constant, but in fact at time t seconds, its position vector,
r metres, is given by:

$$\mathbf{r} = \begin{bmatrix} 10\cos t^2 \\ 10\sin t^2 \end{bmatrix} = 10 \begin{bmatrix} \cos t^2 \\ \sin t^2 \end{bmatrix}$$

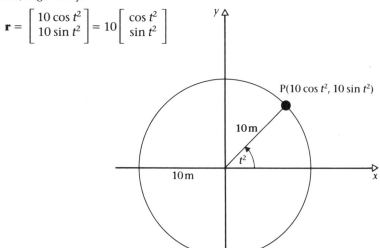

(a) Calculate its velocity vector $\mathbf{v}\,\mathrm{m\,s^{-1}}$.
   Interpret the result.

(b) Calculate its acceleration vector, $\mathbf{a}\,\mathrm{m\,s^{-2}}$, and show that

$$\mathbf{a} = 20 \begin{bmatrix} -\sin t^2 \\ \cos t^2 \end{bmatrix} - 40t^2 \begin{bmatrix} \cos t^2 \\ \sin t^2 \end{bmatrix}$$

Interpret the two parts of this vector as components of acceleration in
the radial and tangential directions (i.e. towards the centre and along
the tangent).

(c) When a particle moves in a circle is the acceleration necessarily towards
the centre?

3.5 Modelling with circular motion

In the exercises, you met many situations which could form the basis for investigation.

Describe the motion in each of the situations above.
What assumptions should you make in each case?
How valid are your assumptions?

What other situations can you think of which might be modelled using the mechanics in this chapter?

After working through this chapter you should:

1   be familiar with examples of motion which can be appropriately measured as the motion of a particle rotating with constant angular speed ω at a distance r from an axis of rotation;

2   know that, for a particle rotating with constant angular speed

  • the velocity of the particle will have magnitude $r\omega$ and the direction of the velocity, although constantly changing, will always be tangential to the circle;

  • the vector acceleration of the particle will have magnitude $r\omega^2$ and the direction (again constantly changing) will always be towards the axis of rotation;

  • the time for one revolution is $T = \dfrac{2\pi}{\omega}$;

3   be able to apply Newton's laws of motion to various situations involving circular motion;

4   know that the acceleration of a particle is in the direction of the resultant force and not necessarily in the direction of motion;

5   know that if a particle is travelling at constant speed it may still have a vector acceleration.

Investigating angular speed

This tasksheet contains two versions of the same experiment. The version you choose will depend on the apparatus you have available.

Version 1

You will need:

- A turntable
- A penny
- A stopwatch

Place the penny on the turntable so that its centre is 0.06 metre from the centre of the turntable. Set the turntable spinning so that it rotates through an angle of 2 radians every second.

1 The angular speed is 2 radians per second. What is this in revolutions per minute (r.p.m.)?

2 What is the speed of the penny in metres per second?

3 What can you say about the velocity of the penny?

4 Where could you place a second penny so that:

(a) its speed is half that of the first penny;

(b) its speed is twice that of the first penny;

(c) its velocity is twice that of the first penny?

The motion of the penny can be plotted on a grid.

5 How long does it take the penny to reach (0, 0.06)?

6 Find the coordinates of the penny after:

(a) 0.25 second;

(b) 0.5 second;

(c) 1 second;

(d) 2 seconds.

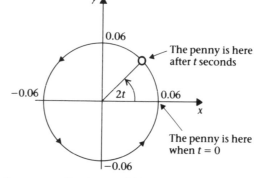

7 What are the coordinates of the penny after t seconds?

Version 2

You will need:

- Two pieces of plastic strip with holes in
- A paper fastener
- Some sugar paper
- A stopwatch

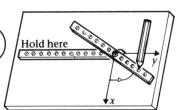

Hold here

1 Fasten two strips together with the paper fastener. Hold the bottom strip firmly on the sugar paper so that the top strip is free to rotate. Put a pencil through a hole, A, 6 cm from the paper fastener. Use the pencil to turn the strip. Can you move your hand at a steady speed so that it takes about 1 second to turn through 2 radians?

2 The angular speed is about 2 radians per second. What is this in revolutions per minute (r.p.m.)?

3 What is the speed of the pencil point in metres per second?

4 What can you say about the velocity of the pencil point?

5 Where could you place your pencil so that the strip still takes 1 second to rotate through 2 radians but:

  (a) the pencil point now travels at half the speed of A;

  (b) the pencil point now travels at twice the speed of A;

  (c) the pencil point travels at twice the velocity of A?

The motion of the pencil point can be plotted on a grid.

6 How long does it take the pencil point to reach (0, 0.06)?

7 Find the coordinates of the pencil point after

  (a) 0.25 second;   (b) 0.5 second;

  (c) 1 second;   (d) 2 seconds.

8 What are the coordinates of your pencil point after t seconds if you continue to turn the strip at the same angular speed?

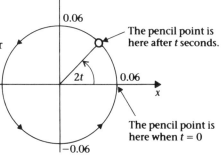

The pencil point is here after t seconds.

The pencil point is here when $t = 0$

Satellites

In 1957, Sputnik I, a round sphere of metal, was blasted off into space by the USSR. It neither fell back to the ground nor disappeared into the depths of space. Instead it remained near the Earth going round and round only a few hundred miles above the ground. It finally fell back to Earth three months later. Since then, many hundreds of satellites have been put into orbit, mostly around the Earth. Craft have been orbited around the Sun, Moon, Mars and other planets in the solar system but these are generally known as **space probes**.

The use of satellites has many practical benefits to humanity. The world's meteorological services depend increasingly on satellite photographs of cloud cover and on measurements of atmospheric properties made from space. They can also be used for pollution and pest control. The pictures that can be obtained are of such good resolution that the swarms of locusts travelling across Africa can be tracked and the information used to combat their menace. Communications satellites are of great importance, not just for relaying television transmissions but also for providing industry and government with the telephone and data links needed. The data gained from scientific satellites has greatly increased people's knowledge and understanding of their planet. The first space laboratory, the Skylab space station, launched in 1973, had a mass of 90 600 kg and a length of 36 metres. It orbited 434 km above the Earth. The drag of the atmosphere gradually slowed it down and in its 34 981st orbit it fell to Earth, burning up over Western Australia.

Many different types of orbit can be achieved depending on the mass of the satellite, the capability of the launch rocket and the angle of the orbit to the equator. The satellite must achieve a velocity of $8450\,\mathrm{m\,s^{-1}}$ to achieve a low orbit, and $11\,170\,\mathrm{m\,s^{-1}}$ to escape from the Earth's pull and go into deep space. By choosing a suitable combination of upward and horizontal thrust, the satellite can be put into any orbit from circular to highly elliptical. The greater the thrust the higher the orbit. The greater the horizontal thrust, the more elliptical the orbit will be. Almost all the world's communications satellites are in circular orbits above the Earth's equator at a height of 35 900 km. A satellite in such an orbit circles the Earth at the same angular speed as the Earth and so it always lies above the same point on the Earth's surface. Not all satellites travel in orbit above the equator. A satellite launched at an angle to the equator will pass over most of the Earth's surface during its life. Satellites used to watch for pollution usually have such an orbit. Most satellites are launched from somewhere near the equator. This means that they can use the velocity of the Earth's surface to help them achieve their orbit.

Although a satellite in orbit should stay in space for ever, this is often not the case. If it is in orbit within a few hundred miles of the Earth's surface the atmosphere will eventually slow the satellite down and it will fall back to Earth. Many satellites are equipped with small booster rockets that can be used to increase their height above the Earth when it reaches a critical point and so extend the life of the satellite. In addition, the Space Shuttle programme has enabled some satellites to be repaired. In April 1984, George Nelson was one of a team of astronauts who jetted from the shuttle to repair the satellite Solar Max, in orbit at a height of 467 km above the Earth. They jokingly named themselves the Ace Satellite repair company. The first Briton in space was Helen Sharman, who spent eight days in the Soviet Union's Mir space station in orbit around the Earth, travelling at a speed of approximately $8450\,\mathrm{m\,s^{-1}}$.

Problem

George Nelson passed over Singapore as he was mending Solar Max. Assuming that the satellite travelled on an orbit above the equator, how many **more** times did he pass over Singapore in the following 24 hours that he stayed on the satellite?

1   Set up a simple mathematical model of the motion of George Nelson as he travelled round the Earth with Solar Max. You should draw a diagram and label it clearly, state any assumptions you make and define any variables you use, obtaining any appropriate constants from the data on the previous page or earlier in the text.

2   Use your model to find his speed and hence find out how many times he passed over Singapore in the 24-hour period.

4 Rigid bodies

4.1 Rotating objects

In the previous chapters of this unit, various objects were modelled, in motion and at rest, by considering them to be particles. There are situations when this model must be extended.

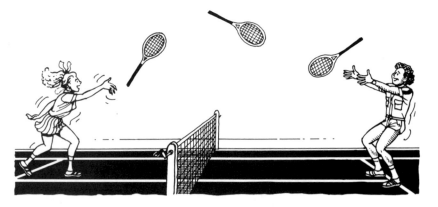

(a) Watch from the side as one person throws a tennis racket through the air to another person, as shown in the picture above. Describe its path. Does it behave like a projectile?

(b) Stick a red dot on the side of the handle and watch the dot as the racket is thrown. Describe the path of the red dot.

(c) Balance the racket horizontally on your finger and place the dot at the balance point. Describe the path of the red dot in this case.

(d) Can you suggest some rules for how any rigid body moves through the air when thrown?

One of the important properties of a particle is that it does not have shape or size. This means that you can think of all the forces as acting at a single point. However, it also means that you cannot take into account any rotational motion which might be caused by the forces.

A **rigid body** is a body which has a fixed size and shape. Where forces act on a body to try to rotate it, you may have to take into account the size and shape of the body in question and model it as a rigid body.

4.2 Moments

Suspend a 1 kg mass from the end of a metre ruler and hold the ruler as shown in the diagram below.

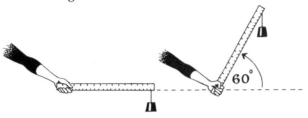

(a) Why is it easier to hold the metre ruler when it is at an angle of 60°?

(b) What does 'easier' mean in this context?

(c) Draw a force diagram for the ruler in each situation. Try to feel where your hand presses up (and down?) on the ruler.

TASKSHEET 1S — Balancing (page 93)

If the effect of a force being applied to an object is to cause it to rotate about a pivot, then this effect is called the **moment of the force about the pivot**. A pivot is a line or axis through a particular point.

The moment of a force about an axis, O, is the product of the magnitude of the force applied and the perpendicular distance between the line of action of the force and the axis, O.

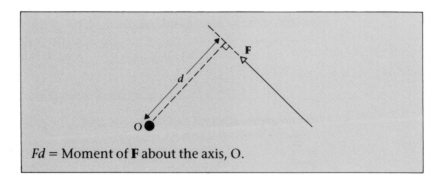

Fd = Moment of **F** about the axis, O.

The sense of a moment is either clockwise or anticlockwise. By convention anticlockwise is taken as positive.

The units of a moment are newton metres (N m).

EXAMPLE 1

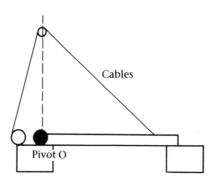

Cables

Pivot O

A drawbridge of mass 500 kg and length 5 m is to be winched into the upright position by two cables. The cables make an angle of 35° with the bridge and are attached to the bridge 4 m from the pivot, O. What is the moment of the weight of the drawbridge about the hinge? If the tension in each cable is 2724 newtons, what is the moment of these forces about the pivot?

SOLUTION

Assume that the bridge is uniform and that the cables are light. There are four forces acting on the bridge when it is on the point of being raised; its weight, the tensions in the two cables and a reaction, **R**, at the hinge. Assume that $g = 10 \text{N kg}^{-1}$.

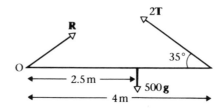

Moment of the weight about the pivot, O = 500g × 2.5 Nm clockwise
                                          = 12500 Nm clockwise

Moment of each cable about the pivot, O = 2724 × 4 sin 35° Nm anticlockwise
                                          = 6250 Nm anticlockwise

> Why is the moment of the force **R** about the pivot equal to zero?

EXERCISE 1

1 Bob and Sally are pushing open an enormous gate hinged at A with forces as shown in the diagram.

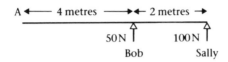

A ◄─── 4 metres ───►◄ 2 metres ►

50 N ↑   100 N ↑
Bob   Sally

Calculate the total turning effect of the forces on the gate about the pivot at A.

2 A light rod OA is pivoted at O as shown. If $P = 6$ newtons, $Q = 7$ newtons and $R = 5$ newtons, find the moments of **P**, **Q** and **R** about the pivot at O.

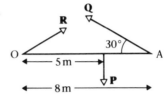

3 A uniform rod OA is pivoted at O and held at an angle ϕ to the vertical (as shown) by a horizontal force P newtons.
If OA = $2a$ metres, find the moment of the weight **W** and the force **P** about the axis through O. (The force at O has been omitted from the diagram.)

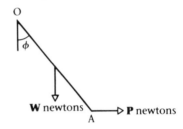

4 Find the moment of each force shown in the diagram about

(a) the pivot point O;

(b) the point A.

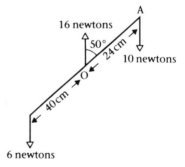

5 A plank of length l is lying horizontally on the ground and is pivoted at one end. Bronwen lifts up the other end with a force **T** newtons at an angle ϕ as shown.

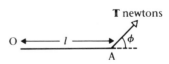

Find the moment of **T** about the pivot O. At what angle should she apply the force in order to maximise the turning effect?

6 Carole lifts a wheelbarrow full of brick rubble (combined mass 90 kg). Estimate the lifting force.

7E Josie and her son Winston are on a swing see-saw. Josie has mass 60 kg and Winston 20 kg. Does the gravitational force acting on Winston or that acting on his mother provide the greater moment about the pivot when the see-saw is in the position shown?

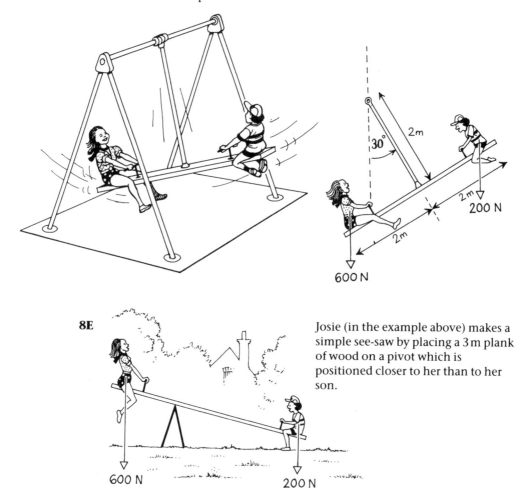

8E Josie (in the example above) makes a simple see-saw by placing a 3 m plank of wood on a pivot which is positioned closer to her than to her son.

(a) How close to Josie should the pivot be placed if the see-saw is to balance?

(b) The plank of wood is quite heavy. Does this make a difference to your answer?

4.3 Equilibrium

A particle is in equilibrium when the vector sum of the forces acting on it is zero. This is not necessarily true for a rigid body.

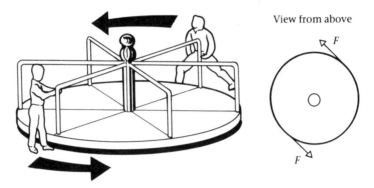

View from above

This section is concerned with the conditions which must be satisfied by the forces acting on a rigid body in equilibrium.

A light rod is suspended at its mid-point from a newton meter. 100 gram and 200 gram weights are attached as shown below and the rod hangs horizontally in equilibrium.

(a) Draw a force diagram for the rod. What would you expect the reading, R, of the newton meter to be?

(b) Apart from the value of R, what else can be deduced from the fact that the rod is in equilibrium?

(c) Can you state what general conditions must be satisfied by the forces acting on a rigid body in equilibrium?

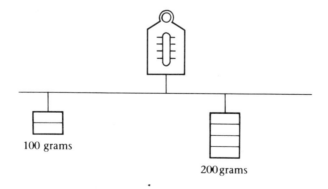

100 grams

200 grams

TASKSHEET 2 — Lines of force (page 94)

A body is in equilibrium when the vector sum of the forces acting on the body is zero **and** the sum of their moments about any axis is zero. If only three forces act on the body then they either pass through a point or are parallel.

For a body which is in equilibrium you can write down equations representing these results.

E X A M P L E 2

A ladder of length 2 m and weight 200 N rests against a smooth vertical wall with its foot on horizontal rough ground, making an angle of 60° with the ground. Find the magnitude of the normal contact force which the wall exerts on the top of the ladder. Find also the magnitude and direction of the contact force exerted by the ground on the foot of the ladder.

S O L U T I O N

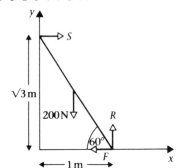

The ladder is in equilibrium so the sum of the forces is zero.

$$\begin{bmatrix} S \\ 0 \end{bmatrix} + \begin{bmatrix} -F \\ 0 \end{bmatrix} + \begin{bmatrix} 0 \\ R \end{bmatrix} + \begin{bmatrix} 0 \\ -200 \end{bmatrix} = 0$$

So $S = F$
and $R = 200$

The sum of the moments of the forces on the ladder about any axis is zero, so taking moments about an axis through the foot of the ladder

$$200 \times \tfrac{1}{2} - S \times \sqrt{3} = 0, \qquad \text{so } S = 57.7$$

The contact force exerted by the wall on the ladder is 57.7 newtons (to 3 s.f.).

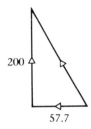

The contact force exerted by the ground on the ladder is $\sqrt{(200^2 + 57.7^2)} = 208$ newtons

at an angle ϕ where $\tan \phi = \dfrac{200}{57.7} \Rightarrow \phi = 74°$

The force is 208 newtons (to 3 s.f.) at an angle of 74° to the horizontal (to the nearest degree).

EXERCISE 2

1   A uniform ruler, supported at the centre, has two masses dangling from it at distances of 10 cm and 7 cm from the centre as shown.

If the rod is horizontal, find an equation linking m_1 and m_2.

Hence find m_2 if $m_1 = 49$.

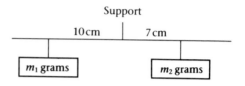

2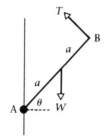

AB is a uniform rod of length $2a$ units hinged to a wall at A and held in equilibrium by a string at B pulling at right angles to the rod.

By taking moments about A, show that

$$T = \tfrac{1}{2} W \cos \theta$$

3   If the angle between the string and BA in question 2 is only 60°, show that the tension required is greater than before.

4   A force $\begin{bmatrix} 3 \\ 4 \end{bmatrix}$ newtons acts at the point (5, 2).

Find the moment of the force about the origin by finding

(a) the sum of the moments of the components about 0,

(b) the moment of the resultant force about 0.

(Hint: graph paper may help.)

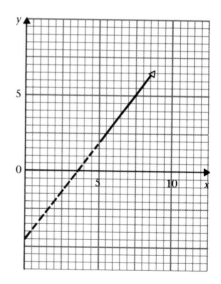

5   Two removal men are carrying a loaded rectangular box at a steady rate up a flight of stairs, inclined at 45° to the horizontal. The loaded box is of weight 750 newtons, its length is 2 m and its square ends have edges of length 0.8 m. Calculate the part of the weight supported by each of the hands of each man if they are holding the underneath of each square end. What assumptions are you making?

What do the results suggest about the position for the stronger man of the two?

6 A car weighing 6800 N has its axles 3 m apart. If its centre of gravity is 1.2 m in front of the rear axle,

(a) what force will be exerted by the road on each wheel? What assumptions are you making?

(b) If luggage of weight 600 N is placed on the roof rack so that its weight acts through the centre of gravity of the car, what force will then be exerted on each wheel by the road?

(c) If the luggage is placed centrally in the boot so that its weight acts at a distance of 0.6 m beyond the rear axle, what force will then be exerted on each wheel by the road?

7E A man's forearm is 0.3 m from the elbow joint to the palm, its weight is 27 N and its centre of gravity is 0.13 m from the joint. The biceps muscle, which raises the forearm, is 0.02 m from the joint. Assume that the forearm is horizontal and the biceps muscle is vertical.

Find the tension in the biceps

(a) when the hand is empty;

(b) when a weight of 45 N is held in the palm.

4.4 Centre of gravity

'Josie is 2 m from the pivot.'

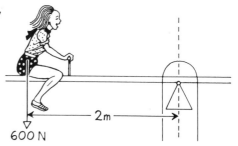

600 N
2 m

A statement like this really means that Josie's **centre of gravity** is 2 m from the pivot. The gravitational pull on the woman acts on all parts of her, but, from the point of view of taking moments about a pivot, the effect of the gravitational pull is that of a single force acting at a point which is called the centre of gravity.

(a) Estimate the approximate positions of the centres of gravity of the gymnast and athlete illustrated below.

(b) In each case, comment on the relevance of your answer to the actions they are performing.

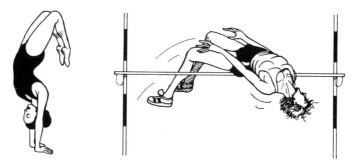

The position of the centre of gravity of the human body is important not only to athletes. Many of the movements you make throughout the day are purely to make small adjustments to the positon of your centre of gravity in order to maintain balance.

You can alter the position of your centre of gravity by changing your shape, but the centre of gravity of a rigid body is a fixed point, no matter what the orientation of the body or how it is moving. Tasksheet 3 will consider how to determine the positions of centres of gravity by experiment.

TASKSHEET 3 — The Fosbury flop (page 95)

The following example illustrates how you can calculate the location of the centre of gravity of a compound object.

EXAMPLE 3

An object consists of a 400 gram mass on one end of a rod and a 100 gram mass on the other. The rod itself is a uniform cylinder of mass 100 grams and length 40 cm. The location of the centres of gravity of the individual masses and of the rod itself are shown on the diagram below, but where is the centre of gravity when the three of them together form 'a single object'?

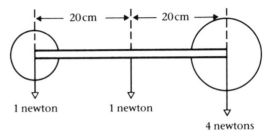

SOLUTION

Suppose the object is pivoted about the left-hand end of the rod.

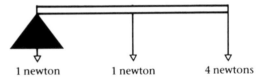

The moment of the 100 gram mass will be zero because its line of action passes through the pivot.

The moment of the 400 gram mass will be $4 \times 0.4 = 1.6$ N m clockwise. The moment of the rod itself will be $1 \times 0.2 = 0.2$ N m clockwise. Thus the total moment about the pivot is 1.8 N m clockwise.

The total gravitational force acting on the object is 6 newtons, so if the centre of gravity is a distance d metres from the pivot, it follows that the moment of the object as a whole about the pivot is $6 \times d$. This must be the same as the sum of the moments of the three parts of the object about the pivot, so

$$6 \times d = 1.8 \Rightarrow d = 0.3$$

The weighted rod will behave as though a single force of 6 newtons was acting at a point 30 cm along its length measured from the 100 gram mass. It is this point, the centre of gravity, which will obey Newton's laws of motion and follow a parabolic path if the rod is thrown.

For the weighted rod of example 3, take the pivot at any point you choose and check that you obtain the same position for the centre of gravity.

The centre of gravity of a compound body is the point at which the total weight of the body can be said to act. If the body is symmetrical, it lies on the line, or lines, of symmetry of the body.

The moment of the weight of the whole body about **any** pivot, O, is equal to the sum of the moments of the weights of the component parts of the body about O.

EXERCISE 3

1   Find the centre of gravity of the following objects.

(a)
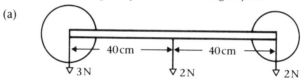

(b)
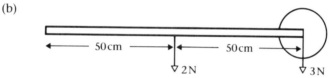

2   The diagram shows a person standing upright with both arms stretched out sideways parallel with the ground.

Axes are drawn with the person facing in the direction of the x-axis, and with the origin vertically below the person's centre of gravity.

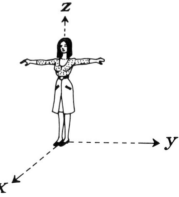

The arms are moved as indicated below. All movements are from the original starting position.

   (i)   Both arms are rotated through 90° to a vertically upward position.

   (ii) The right arm is lowered to a vertically downward position.

   (iii) The left arm is held horizontally outwards towards the front.

   (iv) The left arm is lowered to a vertically downward position and the right arm is held horizontally outwards towards the front.

For each of the movements, describe whether the displacement of the centre of gravity from its **original** position is positive, negative or zero in the direction of the x, y and z axes.

4.5 Centre of mass

A space platform orbiting the Earth consists of three spherical modules attached to a rigid connecting walkway as shown in the diagram. (The walkway is of negligible mass compared with the mass of the modules.) The gravitational force per unit mass is g newtons.

Small booster rockets, used to manoeuvre the platform, are located near the platform's centre of gravity.

In the absence of further information you can assume that

(a) the masses of the three modules are m_1, m_2 and m_3;

(b) the distances of the centres of gravity of the modules are x_1, x_2 and x_3 from the end of the walkway.

You can find the centre of gravity of the space platform by taking moments about the imaginary pivot O shown in the diagram.

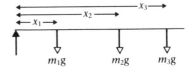

Total moment = $m_1gx_1 + m_2gx_2 + m_3gx_3$ clockwise.

If the centre of gravity is located a distance $\bar{x}$ from O then

$$(m_1g + m_2g + m_3g)\,\bar{x} = m_1gx_1 + m_2gx_2 + m_3gx_3$$

$$\bar{x} = \frac{m_1x_1 + m_2x_2 + m_3x_3}{m_1 + m_2 + m_3} = \frac{\sum mx}{\sum m}$$

(a) Does gravitational attraction make any difference to the position of the platform's centre of gravity in the case above?

(b) What assumption has been made about the gravitational force per unit mass? Is this a reasonable assumption?

TASKSHEET 4 — Average mass (page 97)

In the tasksheet you saw how to calculate the position of the centre of mass of a two-dimensional shape and you saw why it is sensible to refer to the centre of mass as the mean or average position of the mass.

If a body can be modelled as a number of rigidly connected point masses $m_1, m_2, m_3, m_4 \ldots$ located at points $(x_1, y_1), (x_2, y_2) \ldots$ then the centre of mass will be located at $(\bar{x}, \bar{y})$ where

$$\bar{x} = \frac{\sum mx}{\sum m} \qquad \bar{y} = \frac{\sum my}{\sum m}$$

Under normal circumstances the position of the centre of gravity is independent of the gravitational force per unit mass and hence is the same as the position of the centre of mass and can be calculated in the same way. These two terms are used interchangeably.

EXAMPLE 4

A space platform consists of four modules, of masses 1, 2, 3, and 4 tonnes, at the corners A, B, C and D respectively of a light square framework of side a metres. Locate the position of the centre of mass.

SOLUTION

The platform is modelled as four point masses located at $(0, 0), (a, 0), (a, a), (0, a)$.

The centre of mass lies at $(\bar{x}, \bar{y})$ where

$$\bar{x} = \frac{\sum mx}{\sum m} = \frac{1 \times 0 + 2 \times a + 3 \times a + 4 \times 0}{1 + 2 + 3 + 4} = 0.5\,a$$

$$\bar{y} = \frac{\sum my}{\sum m} = \frac{1 \times 0 + 2 \times 0 + 3 \times a + 4 \times a}{1 + 2 + 3 + 4} = 0.7a$$

The centre of mass is at $(0.5a, 0.7a)$

The centres of gravity of many objects are easy to find using symmetry. For example, it is reasonable to assume that the centre of gravity of the Earth is at its geometric centre and the centre of gravity of a rectangular lamina is at its point of symmetry. In other cases, a combination of symmetry and the mean position idea can be used.

EXERCISE   4

1   A balancing toy is made by soldering two spheres of the same uniform density to an L-shaped wire as shown. A small metal pin of negligible mass is to be soldered to the longer arm so that its point is at the centre of gravity of the object.

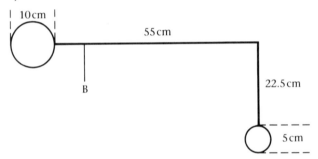

If the mass of the wire can be ignored and the spheres have mass 20 grams and 80 grams find the length and position of the balance pin, B.

2   Find the centre of gravity of each of the following laminae.

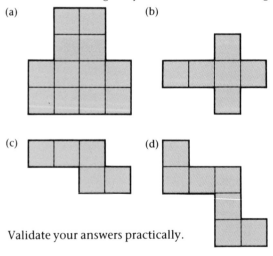

Validate your answers practically.

3   Obtaining suitable data from an encyclopaedia or other source, find the centre of mass of the Earth and Moon together.

4.6 Modelling rigid bodies

There are many situations that can be investigated using the ideas in this chapter. You may have noticed some of them as you worked through the examples.

All the situations in the picture above could be modelled using rigid body mechanics.

What assumptions should you make in each case?
How valid are your assumptions?
What other situations can you think of?

In the opening discussion point of this chapter, you will have observed that the tennis racket rotated about its centre of gravity, whilst the centre of gravity itself followed the parabolic path of a particle.

According to Newton's second law, the change in momentum of a body will be in the direction of the resultant force acting on it. However, it is the centre of gravity which will move in this manner and other parts of the body could be rotating about the centre of gravity. For this reason, it is usual as a first approximation to represent the body as a **point mass** located at the centre of gravity with all the forces acting on the body shown as acting on this point alone. This is what is meant by the term **particle**.

The detailed study of the dynamics and statics of rigid bodies can be followed up in the unit *Modelling with rigid bodies*.

TASKSHEET 5E – *Which slides first? (page 98)*

After working through this chapter you should:

1 know that the moment of a force about a pivot is the product of the magnitude of the force and the distance between the pivot and the line of action of the force (units are usually in newton metres, i.e. Nm);

2 be able to find the total moment of several forces about a pivot by summing the individual moments (by convention, anticlockwise moments are taken as positive and clockwise moments as negative);

3 know that, for an object to be in equilibrium,

   • the sum of the forces acting upon it must be zero;

   • the sum of moments of these forces about any pivot must be zero;

   • if three forces act on the object then they either pass through a point or are parallel;

4 be able to use the equilibrium conditions listed above to solve statics questions;

5 know that the centre of gravity of a body is the point at which the total gravitational force on the body appears to act;

6 be able to find the position of the centre of gravity of an object by using moments and understand that the centre of mass and centre of gravity of an object are normally coincident where

$$(\bar{x}, \bar{y}) = \left(\frac{\sum mx}{\sum m} , \frac{\sum my}{\sum m} \right);$$

7 appreciate that (as a first approximation) it is convenient to model an object as a point mass, at the centre of gravity, with all forces acting at this point;

8 appreciate that the particle model is not always appropriate;

9 know that the centre of gravity of a projectile follows a parabolic path.

Balancing

Use a bulldog clip to suspend a
metre ruler so that it hangs
horizontally.

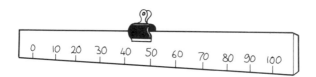

Suspend a 120 gram mass from the 26 cm mark.

1 Find the mass which should be suspended from
the 86 cm mark to balance the ruler in a
horizontal position.

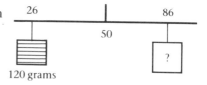

2 Where should a 180 gram mass be suspended
to balance the turning moment of the
120 gram mass?

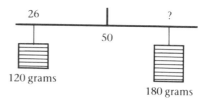

3 A 80 gram mass is suspended from the 61 cm
mark (the 120 gram mass is still at the 26 cm
mark). Where should a 100 gram mass be
suspended to balance the system?

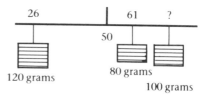

Lines of force

You will need:

- A stiff piece of card with holes punched round the edge
- Four or five pieces of string

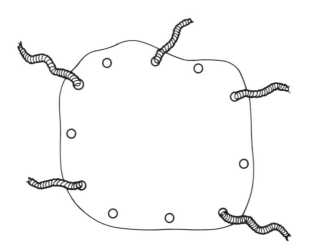

Thread each length of string through a different hole and tie a knot on the underside of the card so that the string swivels freely.

- Take two strings and pull.
- Now pull on three strings.
- What about four strings?
- Describe the lines of action of the forces when the body is in equilibrium.
- Make notes about what you see.

If a rigid body is in equilibrium under the action of three forces is it possible for

(a) the three forces to be parallel;

(b) the lines of action of the forces to lie through a point;

(c) the forces to be non-planar;

(d) neither (a) nor (b) to hold?

What happens if there are four forces acting on the body?

The Fosbury flop

The 'average' human body may be modelled by a series of connected cylinders for the arms, legs and trunk, and a sphere for the head.

The relative proportions of the length and mass will vary considerably from person to person, but a reasonable model is shown.

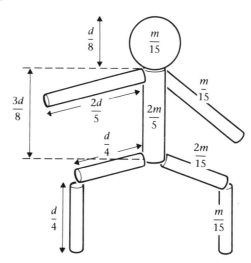

You will probably have seen athletes doing the Fosbury flop in international high-jump competitions. Although the movements through the air are complex, the path of the centre of gravity is parabolic and once the athlete has left the ground there is nothing he or she can do to alter it. The athlete's complicated movements are aimed at 'raising herself' above her centre of gravity as much as possible at the critical point of clearing the bar. It is interesting to investigate her position relative to her centre of gravity at this point in the jump.

Although the whole process is three-dimensional, you can gain a good idea of what is happening by looking at a two-dimensional model as shown in the diagram below. Sketch an enlargement of the drawing onto thick (stiff) card.

Use Blu-Tack to attach coins to the card along the arms, legs and body and on the head to approximate the mass of the high jumper. (2p coins are suitable with one coin per $\frac{1}{15}$th mass.)

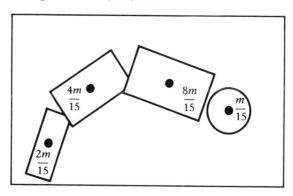

Pin the card to the board in such a way that it is free to swing about the pin. This is the pivot.

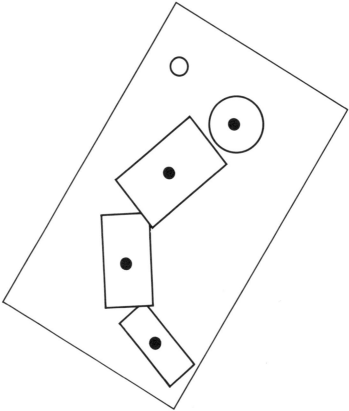

When the card is at rest the centre of gravity will be directly below the pivot. This is because when the line of action of the gravitational force passes through the pivot the moment of the force is zero, so there is no rotation about the pivot.

If you draw a line vertically down from the pivot, the centre of gravity must be somewhere on this line. If you repeat this process from different pivot points, the lines you draw will intersect at the centre of gravity. (The accuracy will depend on how accurate your vertical lines are.)

Once you have identified the position of the centre of gravity, what do you expect to happen if you pivot the card about an axis through this point? Try it and see.

On the other side of the card draw a model of someone, for example, bending down to touch her toes, doing a dive, or performing a gymnastic movement, and identify the position of the centre of gravity.

Average mass

A group of students were about to test a model bridge to destruction by gradually increasing the weight placed on the centre span. Before the test they were asked to predict the maximum weight the bridge could carry.
The information gathered is shown in the histogram below.

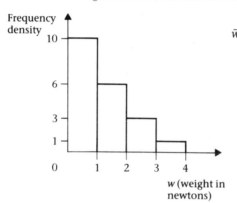

$$\bar{w} = \frac{\sum fw}{\sum f}$$

$$= \frac{10 \times 0.5 + 6 \times 1.5 + 3 \times 2.5 + 1 \times 3.5}{10 + 6 + 3 + 1}$$

$$= \frac{25}{20}$$

$$= 1.25$$

1 Draw a histogram on stiff card, using a scale of 2 cm per unit for the x-axis and 1 cm per unit for the y-axis, and cut it out.

The centre of gravity of the resulting lamina is situated at $(\bar{x}, \bar{y})$.

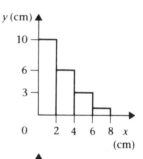

Locate the centre of gravity of the lamina by balancing it on the edge of a table or suspending it from a pin.

2 By modelling each rectangle as a point mass at its centre, the location of the centre of gravity can be calculated taking moments about the pivot shown in the diagram.

$$\bar{x} = \frac{10 \times 1 + 6 \times 3 + 3 \times 5 + 1 \times 7}{10 + 6 + 3 + 1} = \frac{50}{20} = 2.5$$

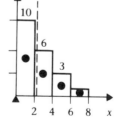

Turn the lamina round so that the y-axis is horizontal and use the same technique to find $\bar{y}$.

3 In what sense is the point $(\bar{x}, \bar{y})$ the mean of the lamina?

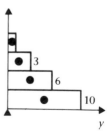

Which slides first?

Balance a long length of track on your fingers as shown, and gradually begin to draw your hands together. What happens?

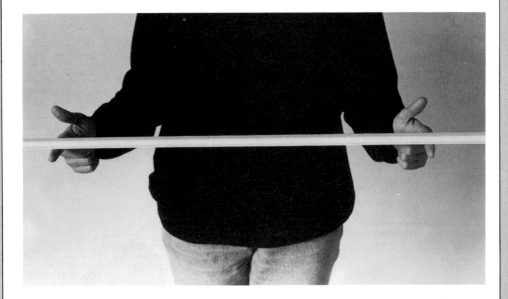

- Which finger slides first?
- What happens to the track?
- Where do your fingers finish?
- Do both your fingers slide at once?
- What happens if you use a pencil or a rubber instead of one of your fingers?

Model the situation mathematically and explain all the features observed.

5 Extended investigations

5.1 What is an extended investigation?

If you look back at what you have done so far, you will see that you were given clearly defined problems to solve. For example:

- How many buses can Eddie Kidd jump over?
- What is the radius of the orbit of a geostatic satellite?
- Will the block slide down the slope?

In each case you set up a model, analysed it mathematically using Newtonian mechanics, interpreted your results in plain English, finally validating your results practically, if possible. Because the problems occurred in specific areas of the text, it has been clear which parts of Newtonian mechanics were expected to be relevant.

At the end of each chapter some situations have been suggested for extended modelling investigations.

It is not always obvious how Newtonian mechanics can be applied in such situations. There is an art in **observing** relevant features and then identifying problems to solve. Identifying an appropriate problem to solve is the starting point for an extended modelling investigation.

5.2 Getting started

To get you started, you are going to look at how some students tackled an extended investigation, 'Design a children's slide'.

By using simple apparatus, by going to look at a slide or by simply sitting and thinking, write down anything that needs to be taken into account if you have the task of designing a children's slide.

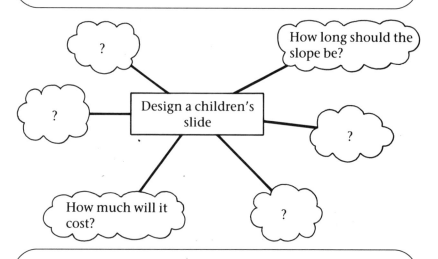

Compare your list with the samples of students' work given in the solutions.

You will probably notice some differences, but there will be many similarities. You are now ready to go on to the next stage.

Identify those problems that you think you can solve or model by using Newtonian mechanics.

Compare your list with those in the solutions.

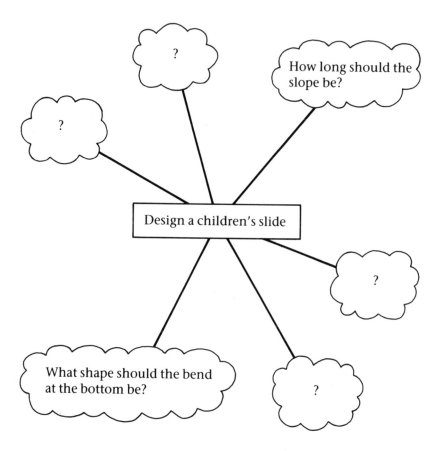

You have broken down the original problem into smaller ones and identified those problems you can solve using the mathematics developed in the unit. You could now identify variables, set up a model, analyse the sub-problems and interpret and validate your solutions.

The final stage would be to collect together your conclusions and write a detailed report.

5.3 Your own investigation

- Decide on your investigation. It should be one which interests you. (You will find ideas at the end of each chapter.)

- List the general features of the subject which occur to you.

- Identify those features which you can model and those which you cannot.

- Define the variables for those problems you think you can model and consider whether they raise further problems.

- Solve these problems.

- Interpret and validate your conclusions.

- Write up your investigation.

  Good luck!

After working through this chapter you should:

1 understand how to divide your investigation into manageable parts;

2 be able to solve each relevant problem using Newtonian mechanics;

3 have chosen and completed your own investigation, and written up your conclusions.

Solutions

1 Projectiles

1.1 Weight

E X E R C I S E   1   *(All answers are given to 3 significant figures.)*

1 $F = \dfrac{Gm_1m_2}{r^2} = \dfrac{6.67 \times 10^{-11} \times 1 \times 1.5}{1}$ N

$= 1.00 \times 10^{-10}$ N

They do not accelerate towards one another because the force of attraction is opposed by friction forces.

2 $F = 9.8m$ N
$= 39.2$ N

Change in momentum each second is 39.2 kg m s^{-1}
Change in momentum $= 3 \times 39.2 = 117.6 \text{ kg m s}^{-1}$
The Earth's change in momentum $= 117.6 \text{ kg m s}^{-1}$

Therefore its change in velocity $= \dfrac{117.6}{5.98 \times 10^{24}}$

$= 1.97 \times 10^{-23} \text{ m s}^{-1}$ (to 3 s.f.) which is negligible.

3 (a) Momentum after t seconds $= 5 \times 49 = 245 \text{ kg m s}^{-1}$
Change in momentum after t seconds $= 245 \text{ kg m s}^{-1}$
Force $= 5g = 5 \times 9.8 = 49$

Change in momentum produced by the force in t seconds $= 49t \text{ kg m s}^{-1}$

(b) $245 = 49t$
$\Rightarrow \quad t = 5$ seconds

(c) Displacement $=$ area under a (velocity, time) graph

$= \dfrac{5 \times 49}{2}$

$= 122.5$ metres

The distance fallen is 122.5 metres.

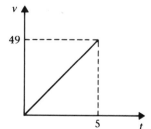

4 Change in momentum in 4 seconds $= 78.4 \, \mathrm{kg \, m \, s^{-1}}$

Force $= mg = 9.8m \, \mathrm{N}$

$\Rightarrow$ Change in momentum in 4 seconds $= 4 \times 9.8m = 39.2m \, \mathrm{kg \, m \, s^{-1}}$

$\Rightarrow 78.4 = 39.2m$

$\Rightarrow \quad m = 2 \, \mathrm{kg}$

Change in momentum = final momentum − initial momentum

$\Rightarrow 78.4 = mv - mu$

$\quad 78.4 = 2v - 0$

$\Rightarrow \quad v = 39.2 \, \mathrm{m \, s^{-1}}$

5 (a) (i) Since the radius of the Earth is only to 4 significant figures, i.e. to the nearest kilometre, the weight at the top of the Eiffel Tower is the same as at the Earth's surface, 9.80 N to the nearest 3 significant figures.

(ii) At the top of Mount Everest, the distance from the centre of the Earth is

$d = 6.387 \times 10^6$ metres

So weight $= \dfrac{GMm}{d^2} = \dfrac{6.673 \times 10^{-11} \times 5.974 \times 10^{24}}{6.387^2 \times 10^{12}}$

$= 9.77$ newtons

(iii) At height 928 km, the distance from the centre of the Earth is

$d = (6.378 + 0.928) \times 10^6 = 7.31 \times 10^6$ metres

So weight $= \dfrac{GMm}{d^2} = \dfrac{6.673 \times 10^{-11} \times 5.974 \times 10^{24}}{7.31^2 \times 10^{12}} = 7.46$ newtons

(b) Let r be the radius of the Earth.

Weight $= \dfrac{GMm}{(2r)^2}$

Since $\dfrac{GMm}{r^2} = 9.8$, weight $= \dfrac{9.8}{4} = 2.45$ newtons

(c)

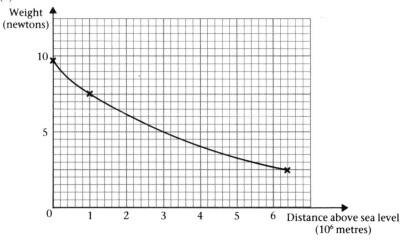

6   Defining upwards as positive,
For the first instant, initial momentum $= 3 \times 49\ \ = 147\,\mathrm{kg\,m\,s^{-1}}$
final momentum $\ \ = 3 \times 9.8 = 29.4\,\mathrm{kg\,m\,s^{-1}}$

Change in momentum in t_1 seconds $= 29.4 - 147$
$$= -117.6\,\mathrm{kg\,m\,s^{-1}}$$

Force $= -3g = -3 \times 9.8 = -29.4\,\mathrm{kg\,m\,s^{-1}}$
Change in momentum in t_1 seconds $= -29.4t_1$
$\Rightarrow\ \ -29.4t_1 = -117.6$
$\Rightarrow\qquad t_1 = .4$ seconds

For the second instant, initial momentum $= 3 \times 49\ \ \ = 147\,\mathrm{kg\,m\,s^{-1}}$
final momentum $\ \ = 3 \times -9.8 = -29.4\,\mathrm{kg\,m\,s^{-1}}$

Change in momentum in t_2 seconds $= -29.4 - 147$
$$= -176.4\,\mathrm{kg\,m\,s^{-1}}$$

Force $= -3g = -29.4\,\mathrm{kg\,m\,s^{-1}}$
Change in momentum in t_2 seconds $= -29.4t_2\,\mathrm{kg\,m\,s^{-1}}$
$\Rightarrow\ -29.4t_2 = -176.4$
$\Rightarrow\qquad t_2 = 6$ seconds

7E   Net force downwards $= 70g - F$
$$= 686 - F$$

Change in momentum after 4 seconds $= (686 - F)4$
$$= (2744 - 4F)\,\mathrm{kg\,m\,s^{-1}}$$

Change in momentum $= mv - mu$
$$= 70 \times 24.5 - 0$$
$$= 1715\,\mathrm{kg\,m\,s^{-1}}$$
$\Rightarrow\qquad\qquad 1715 = 2744 - 4F$
$\Rightarrow\qquad\qquad F = 257$ newtons to 3 s.f.

1.3   Velocity

Complete the formula for Eddie's position at time t.
$$\begin{bmatrix} x \\ y \end{bmatrix} = \begin{bmatrix} ? \\ 9t - 5t^2 \end{bmatrix}$$
Check that your formula fits the data given above.

$$\begin{bmatrix} x \\ y \end{bmatrix} = \begin{bmatrix} 30t \\ 9t - 5t^2 \end{bmatrix}$$

EXERCISE 2

1 If $\mathbf{r} = \begin{bmatrix} 10t \\ 30t - 5t^2 \end{bmatrix}$ then $\mathbf{v} = \begin{bmatrix} 10 \\ 30 - 10t \end{bmatrix}$

(a) $\dfrac{dy}{dt} = 0$ when $t = 3$

(b) When $t = 3$, $\mathbf{v} = \begin{bmatrix} 10 \\ 0 \end{bmatrix}$ and $\mathbf{r} = \begin{bmatrix} 30 \\ 45 \end{bmatrix}$

so the maximum height = 45 metres

(c) When $t = 6$, $\mathbf{r} = \begin{bmatrix} 60 \\ 0 \end{bmatrix}$

so the range = 60 metres

2 (a) At $t = 0$, $\mathbf{v} = \begin{bmatrix} 30 \\ 9 \end{bmatrix}$

so speed $= \sqrt{(30^2 + 9^2)} = 31.3\,\mathrm{m\,s}^{-1}$

(b) When $t = 0.9$, $\mathbf{v} = \begin{bmatrix} 30 \\ 0 \end{bmatrix}$

so speed $= 30\,\mathrm{m\,s}^{-1}$

3 $\mathbf{r} = \begin{bmatrix} 10t \\ 9t - 5t^2 + 2 \end{bmatrix}$

(a) Height of the net above the ground = 2 m

When $y = 2$, $9t - 5t^2 + 2 = 2$

$\Rightarrow\ 9t - 5t^2 = 0$

$\Rightarrow\ t = 0$ or $t = \tfrac{9}{5}$

When $t = \tfrac{9}{5}$, $x = 10t = 18\,\mathrm{m}$

The net should be placed with its centre at $\begin{bmatrix} 18 \\ 2 \end{bmatrix}$.

(b) $\mathbf{v} = \begin{bmatrix} 10 \\ 9 - 10t \end{bmatrix}$

When $t = \dfrac{9}{5}$, $\mathbf{v} = \begin{bmatrix} 10 \\ -9 \end{bmatrix}$

The speed is $13.5\,\mathrm{m\,s}^{-1}$ to 3 significant figures.

4 $\mathbf{r} = \begin{bmatrix} 10t \\ 2 + 10t - 5t^2 \end{bmatrix}$

(a) $\dfrac{d\mathbf{r}}{dt} = \begin{bmatrix} 10 \\ 10 - 10t \end{bmatrix}$

$\Rightarrow$ velocity of projection $= \begin{bmatrix} 10 \\ 10 \end{bmatrix}$

$\Rightarrow$ magnitude $= 10\sqrt{2}\,\mathrm{m\,s}^{-1}$,   direction = 45° to the horizontal

(b) $\dfrac{d^2\mathbf{r}}{dt^2} = \begin{bmatrix} 0 \\ -10 \end{bmatrix}$

Acceleration $= 10\,\text{m s}^{-1}$ downwards

(c) $t = 0,\ \mathbf{r} = \begin{bmatrix} 0 \\ 2 \end{bmatrix}$

The height of release above ground is 2 metres.

(d) The shot hits the ground when $2 + 10t - 5t^2 = 0$

$$\text{i.e. } t = \dfrac{10 + \sqrt{(100 + 40)}}{10}$$
$$= 2.18 \text{ seconds (2 d.p.)}$$
Length $= 10 \times 2.18 = 21.8\,\text{m}$

(e) $\dfrac{d\mathbf{r}}{dt} = \begin{bmatrix} 10 \\ 10 - 10t \end{bmatrix} = \begin{bmatrix} 10 \\ 10 - 21.8 \end{bmatrix} = \begin{bmatrix} 10 \\ -11.8 \end{bmatrix}$ on striking the ground.

(f) $\dfrac{d\mathbf{r}}{dt} = \begin{bmatrix} 10 \\ 10 - 10t \end{bmatrix}$. It is moving horizontally when $10 - 10t = 0$

It moves horizontally when $t = 1$ second. It is then at its maximum height.

(g) Height $= 2 + 10t - 5t^2 = 1 + 10 - 5 = 7\,\text{m}$ when $t = 1$

5 $\mathbf{r} = \begin{bmatrix} 0.5 + 10t \\ 0.75 + 2.8t - 5t^2 \end{bmatrix}$

(a) $\dfrac{d\mathbf{r}}{dt} = \begin{bmatrix} 10 \\ 2.8 - 10t \end{bmatrix}$ initial velocity $= \begin{bmatrix} 10 \\ 2.8 \end{bmatrix}\text{m s}^{-1}$

(b) $t = 0$ on take-off $\mathbf{r} = \begin{bmatrix} 0.5 \\ 0.75 \end{bmatrix}$ metres

i.e. the centre of gravity is in front of the take-off board.

(c) On landing, $0.75 + 2.8t - 5t^2 = 0.75$
$$\Rightarrow t(2.8 - 5t) = 0$$
$$\Rightarrow t = 0 \quad \text{or} \quad t = \dfrac{2.8}{5} = 0.56 \text{ seconds}$$
Length of jump $= 0.5 + 10 \times 0.56$ seconds
$$= 6.1 \text{ metres}$$

1.4 Acceleration under a constant force

(a) Explain how the result above can be expressed as

$$\frac{d\mathbf{v}}{dt} = \begin{bmatrix} 0 \\ -10 \end{bmatrix}.$$

(b) Check this result for Eddie Kidd's motion starting from

$$\mathbf{r} = \begin{bmatrix} 30t \\ 9t - 5t^2 \end{bmatrix}.$$

The change in velocity each second is always constant at $10\,\mathrm{m\,s^{-1}}$ downwards.

so $\dfrac{d\mathbf{v}}{dt} = \begin{bmatrix} 0 \\ -10 \end{bmatrix}$

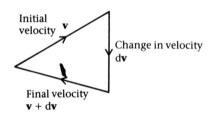

But $\mathbf{v} = \dfrac{d\mathbf{r}}{dt} = \begin{bmatrix} 30 \\ 9 - 10t \end{bmatrix}$

which also gives $\dfrac{d\mathbf{v}}{dt} = \begin{bmatrix} 0 \\ -10 \end{bmatrix}$

EXERCISE 3

1 $\mathbf{r} = \begin{bmatrix} 5t \\ 6t - 5t^2 + 1 \end{bmatrix}$ metres

$\mathbf{v} = \begin{bmatrix} 5 \\ 6 - 10t \end{bmatrix}\mathrm{m\,s^{-1}}$

$\mathbf{a} = \begin{bmatrix} 0 \\ -10 \end{bmatrix}\mathrm{m\,s^{-2}}$

2 $\mathbf{r} = \begin{bmatrix} 9t - t^2 \\ 9t - t^2 + 1 \end{bmatrix}$ metres

$\mathbf{v} = \begin{bmatrix} 9 - 2t \\ 9 - 2t \end{bmatrix}\mathrm{m\,s^{-1}}$

$\mathbf{a} = \begin{bmatrix} -2 \\ -2 \end{bmatrix}\mathrm{m\,s^{-2}}$

$\mathbf{F} = m\mathbf{a} \Rightarrow \mathbf{F} = \begin{bmatrix} -0.2 \\ -0.2 \end{bmatrix}$ newtons

3 $\mathbf{r} = \begin{bmatrix} 5t - t^2 \\ 3 + 5t - t^2 \end{bmatrix}$

$\mathbf{v} = \begin{bmatrix} 5 - 2t \\ 5 - 2t \end{bmatrix}$

$\mathbf{a} = \begin{bmatrix} -2 \\ -2 \end{bmatrix} \Rightarrow \mathbf{F} = m\mathbf{a} = 70 \begin{bmatrix} -2 \\ -2 \end{bmatrix} = \begin{bmatrix} -140 \\ -140 \end{bmatrix}$

4 $\mathbf{r} = \begin{bmatrix} 3t^2 \\ 4t^2 \end{bmatrix}$ $\mathbf{v} = \begin{bmatrix} 6t \\ 8t \end{bmatrix}$ $\mathbf{a} = \begin{bmatrix} 6 \\ 8 \end{bmatrix}$

$\Rightarrow \mathbf{F} = 0.5 \begin{bmatrix} 6 \\ 8 \end{bmatrix} = \begin{bmatrix} 3 \\ 4 \end{bmatrix}$

$\Rightarrow F = 5\,\text{N}$ at an angle $\tan^{-1}\frac{4}{3}$ to the x-axis

5E (a) $\mathbf{a} = \begin{bmatrix} 0 \\ 2 \end{bmatrix}$

$\mathbf{a} = \begin{bmatrix} 0 \\ 2 \end{bmatrix}$ when $t = 2$

(b) $\mathbf{a} = \begin{bmatrix} 0 \\ -8t^{-3} \end{bmatrix}$

$\mathbf{a} = \begin{bmatrix} 0 \\ -1 \end{bmatrix}$ when $t = 2$

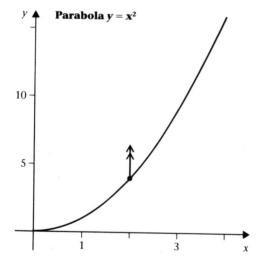

Parabola $y = x^2$

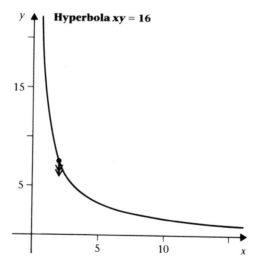

Hyperbola $xy = 16$

(c) $\mathbf{a} = \begin{bmatrix} -\cos t \\ -\sin t \end{bmatrix}$

(d) $\mathbf{a} = \begin{bmatrix} 0 \\ 0 \end{bmatrix}$

$\mathbf{a} = \begin{bmatrix} 0.42 \\ -0.91 \end{bmatrix}$ when $t = 2$

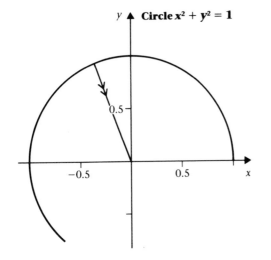

Circle $x^2 + y^2 = 1$

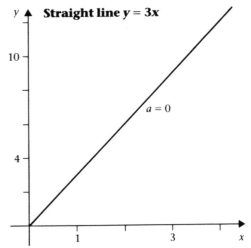

Straight line $y = 3x$

$a = 0$

1.5 Projectile motion

EXERCISE 4

1 Initial velocity $= \begin{bmatrix} 7 \\ 5 \end{bmatrix}$ m s^{-1} $\Rightarrow$ displacement $= \begin{bmatrix} 7t \\ 5t - 5t^2 \end{bmatrix}$ metres

The ball is caught when $5t - 5t^2 = 0 \Rightarrow t = 1$ second

They are 7 metres apart.

2 $\mathbf{a} = \begin{bmatrix} 0 \\ -g \end{bmatrix} = \begin{bmatrix} 0 \\ -10 \end{bmatrix}$

$\Rightarrow \mathbf{v} = \begin{bmatrix} 3 \\ 5 - 10t \end{bmatrix}$

$\Rightarrow \mathbf{r} = \begin{bmatrix} 3t \\ 1 + 5t - 5t^2 \end{bmatrix}$

At maximum height, $5 - 10t = 0$

$\Rightarrow t = 0.5$

Maximum height $= 1 + 5 \times 0.5 - 5 \times 0.25$

$= 3.5 - 1.25$

$= 2.25\,\text{m}$

3 $\mathbf{a} = \begin{bmatrix} 0 \\ -g \end{bmatrix} = \begin{bmatrix} 0 \\ -10 \end{bmatrix}$

$\mathbf{v} = \begin{bmatrix} 21 \cos 40 \\ 21 \sin 40 - 10t \end{bmatrix} = \begin{bmatrix} 16.1 \\ 13.5 - 10t \end{bmatrix}$

$\mathbf{r} = \begin{bmatrix} 21 \cos 40t \\ 2 + 21 \sin 40t - 5t^2 \end{bmatrix} = \begin{bmatrix} 16.1t \\ 2 + 13.5t - 5t^2 \end{bmatrix}$

For length of throw, $2 + 13.5t - 5t^2 = 0$

i.e. $t = \dfrac{13.5 \pm \sqrt{(13.5^2 + 4 \times 5 \times 2)}}{10}$

$= \dfrac{13.5 + 14.91}{10}$

$= \dfrac{28.41}{10} = 2.84$ seconds

The length of the throw is 45.7 m

4E (a) $\mathbf{v} = \begin{bmatrix} 4 \\ 5 - gt \end{bmatrix} = \begin{bmatrix} 4 \\ 5 - 10t \end{bmatrix} \mathrm{m\,s^{-1}}$

$\mathbf{r} = \begin{bmatrix} 4t \\ 5t - 5t^2 \end{bmatrix} \mathrm{m}$

When $t = 2$, $\mathbf{r} = \begin{bmatrix} 8 \\ -10 \end{bmatrix}$ m and the cannon ball is at A.

Furthermore, when $t = 2$, $\mathbf{v} = \begin{bmatrix} 4 \\ 5 - 20 \end{bmatrix} = \begin{bmatrix} 4 \\ -15 \end{bmatrix} \mathrm{m\,s^{-1}}$

(b) Let the rebound velocity be **V**. The momentum is conserved.

So $8 \times \begin{bmatrix} 4 \\ -15 \end{bmatrix} = 8 \times \mathbf{V} + 48 \times \begin{bmatrix} 0 \\ -3 \end{bmatrix}$

$\Rightarrow \mathbf{V} = \dfrac{1}{8} \begin{bmatrix} 32 \\ -120 + 3 \times 48 \end{bmatrix} = \begin{bmatrix} 4 \\ 3 \end{bmatrix}$

(c) After a further t seconds, the ball's velocity is

$\mathbf{v} = \begin{bmatrix} 4 \\ 3 - 10t \end{bmatrix}$

and $\mathbf{r} = \begin{bmatrix} 8 \\ -10 \end{bmatrix} + \begin{bmatrix} 4t \\ 3t - 5t^2 \end{bmatrix}$

Now $3t - 5t^2 = -2$ when $5t^2 - 3t - 2 = 0$ or $t = \dfrac{3 \pm \sqrt{(9 + 40)}}{10} = 1$ or -0.4

so when $t = 1$, $\mathbf{r} = \begin{bmatrix} 8 + 4 \\ -10 + -2 \end{bmatrix} = \begin{bmatrix} 12 \\ -12 \end{bmatrix}$

This takes the cannon-ball clear of the water hazard.

1.6   The general case

(a) Find by integration a vector equation giving the velocity **v** at time t.

(b) By integrating again show that the position vector **r** is given by

$$\mathbf{r} = \begin{bmatrix} u_x t + a \\ -\tfrac{1}{2} g t^2 + u_y t + b \end{bmatrix}$$

(a) $\dfrac{d\mathbf{v}}{dt} = \begin{bmatrix} 0 \\ -g \end{bmatrix}$

$\mathbf{v} = \begin{bmatrix} u_x \\ -gt + u_y \end{bmatrix}$ where $\mathbf{v} = \begin{bmatrix} u_x \\ u_y \end{bmatrix}$ when $t = 0$

(b) But $\mathbf{v} = \dfrac{d\mathbf{r}}{dt}$

$\Rightarrow \mathbf{r} = \begin{bmatrix} u_x t + a \\ -\tfrac{1}{2} g t^2 + u_y t + b \end{bmatrix}$ where $\mathbf{r} = \begin{bmatrix} a \\ b \end{bmatrix}$ when $t = 0$

(a) When $t = \dfrac{2u \sin \phi}{g}$, calculate **r**.

(b) Interpret your result. How can it be validated?

(c) At the highest point on the path of a projectile, the vertical component of the velocity is zero. Use this fact to find an expression, in terms of u, g, and ϕ, for the time taken to reach the highest point.

(d) Use this result to show that the height reached is $\dfrac{u^2 \sin^2 \phi}{2g}$.

(e) Interpret this result as u and ϕ vary. Validate it practically.

(a) When $t = \dfrac{2u \sin \phi}{g}$ $\mathbf{r} = \begin{bmatrix} \dfrac{2u \sin \phi \times u \cos \phi}{g} \\[4mm] \dfrac{2u \sin \phi \times u \sin \phi}{g} - \dfrac{g(2u \sin \phi)^2}{2g^2} \end{bmatrix}$

$= \begin{bmatrix} \dfrac{2u^2 \sin \phi \cos \phi}{g} \\[4mm] 0 \end{bmatrix} = \begin{bmatrix} \dfrac{u^2 \sin 2\phi}{g} \\[4mm] 0 \end{bmatrix}$

(b) When $y = 0$, $x = \dfrac{u^2 \sin 2\phi}{g}$. This is called the range, R. Interpreting

this, you will find that R increases from 0 to $\dfrac{u^2}{g}$ as ϕ increases from

0 to $45°$. Once ϕ has passed $45°$ then $\sin 2\phi$ starts to decrease again.

Sin $2\phi = \sin 2(90 - \phi)$ so the same horizontal distance can be gained by firing either at an angle ϕ or its complementary angle.

The range varies as the square of the velocity for any angle of projection. So if you double the velocity of projection, you multiply the range by 4.

(c) $\mathbf{v} = \begin{bmatrix} u \cos \phi \\ u \sin \phi - gt \end{bmatrix}$

At the highest point, $t = \dfrac{u \sin \phi}{g}$, i.e. $\mathbf{v} = \begin{bmatrix} u \cos \phi \\ 0 \end{bmatrix}$.

(d) $\mathbf{r} = \begin{bmatrix} \dfrac{u^2 \sin 2\phi}{2g} \\ \dfrac{u^2 \sin^2 \phi}{2g} \end{bmatrix}$

and the greatest height reached $= \dfrac{u^2 \sin^2 \phi}{2g}$.

(e) As the speed of projection increases so does the maximum height gained. As the angle of projection increases so does the maximum height gained. This reaches its highest value when the object is thrown vertically upwards.

EXERCISE 5

1 They all land on the floor at the same time. In fact they always have the same height.

2 $\mathbf{v} = \begin{bmatrix} 15 \\ 20 - 10t \end{bmatrix} \mathrm{m\,s^{-1}}$ $\qquad \mathbf{r} = \begin{bmatrix} 15t \\ 20t - 5t^2 \end{bmatrix}$ metres

(a) When $t = 2$, $\mathbf{v} = \begin{bmatrix} 15 \\ 0 \end{bmatrix} \mathrm{m\,s^{-1}}$ and $\mathbf{r} = \begin{bmatrix} 30 \\ 20 \end{bmatrix}$ metres

so it rises to a height of 20 metres.

(b) When $t = 4$, $\mathbf{r} = \begin{bmatrix} 60 \\ 0 \end{bmatrix}$ metres and it bounces 60 m away.

3

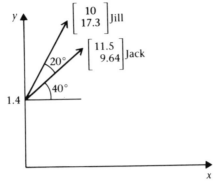

Jill's stone has velocity and displacement

$$\mathbf{v} = \begin{bmatrix} 10 \\ 17.3 - 10t \end{bmatrix} \text{ms}^{-1}, \qquad \mathbf{r} = \begin{bmatrix} 10t \\ 17.3t - 5t^2 + 1.4 \end{bmatrix} \text{metres}$$

Jack's stone has velocity and displacement

$$\mathbf{v} = \begin{bmatrix} 11.5 \\ 9.64 - 10t \end{bmatrix} \text{ms}^{-1}, \qquad \mathbf{r} = \begin{bmatrix} 11.5t \\ 9.64t - 5t^2 + 1.4 \end{bmatrix} \text{metres}$$

(a) When Jill's stone is at its highest point $\mathbf{v} = \begin{bmatrix} 10 \\ 0 \end{bmatrix}$ $\Rightarrow$ $t = 1.73$.

Her stone rises to $t(17.3 - 5t) = 15$ metres.

(b) Jill: Her stone lands when $1.4 + 17.3t - 5t^2 = 0$
$t = 3.54$ or -0.08 so Jill's stone lands after 3.54 seconds.

Jack: His stone lands when $1.4 + 9.64t - 5t^2 = 0$
$t = 2.06$ or -0.13
so his stone lands after 2.06 seconds.

Jack's stone lands first.

(c) Jill: Horizontal distance $= 10t$ $= 35.4$ metres
Jack: Horizontal distance $= 11.5t = 23.7$ metres

Jill's stone lands furthest away.

4   (a) Set up the model: Ignore air resistance.
Let the trees be d metres away.

Analysis: The velocity of the package is $\begin{bmatrix} 30 \\ -10t \end{bmatrix} \text{ms}^{-1}$

so $\begin{bmatrix} x \\ y \end{bmatrix} = \begin{bmatrix} 30t \\ 210 - 5t^2 \end{bmatrix}$ metres

After T seconds, $30T = d$ and $210 - 5T^2 = 30$
$T = 6$ seconds and $d = 180$ metres

(b) Let the package land D metres from the release point after T seconds.
Then $30T = D$ and $210 - 5T^2 = 0$
$T \approx 6.48$ and $D = 194.4$
The package lands 14.4 metres beyond the trees.

5 Let the initial velocity be $\mathbf{u} = \begin{bmatrix} u_x \\ u_y \end{bmatrix}$

so after 5 seconds $\mathbf{r} = \begin{bmatrix} 5u_x \\ 5u_y - 4.9 \times 25 \end{bmatrix} = \begin{bmatrix} 80 \\ 0 \end{bmatrix}$

$5u_x = 80 \Rightarrow u_x = 16$

$5u_y - 4.9 \times 25 = 0 \Rightarrow u_y = 4.9 \times 5 = 24.5$

The initial velocity is $\begin{bmatrix} 16 \\ 24.5 \end{bmatrix} \text{m s}^{-1}$.

6 The maximum range for a projectile occurs when the angle of projection is 45°.

You should look this up yourself. You could try the *Guinness Book of Records*.

Substituting your value for the distance into the equation $u^2 = g \times$ distance will allow you to check your estimation. Remember, however, that this is still just an approximation as the ball did not leave the cricketer's hand at ground level.

7 Let initial speed of the ball be V

So $\mathbf{v} = \begin{bmatrix} V \cos 40° \\ V \sin 40° - 10t \end{bmatrix} \text{m s}^{-1}$

$\mathbf{r} = \begin{bmatrix} Vt \cos 40° \\ Vt \sin 40° - 5t^2 \end{bmatrix}$ metres

so $\begin{bmatrix} Vt \cos 40° \\ Vt \sin 40° - 5t^2 \end{bmatrix} = \begin{bmatrix} 12 \\ 4 \end{bmatrix}$

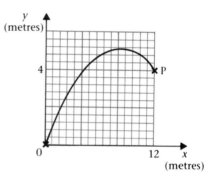

$Vt \cos 40° = 12$

$\Rightarrow t = \dfrac{15.7}{V}$

$Vt \sin 40° - 5t^2 = 4$

Substituting for t, $10.1 - \dfrac{1227}{V^2} = 4$

$\Rightarrow 6.1V^2 = 1227$

$\Rightarrow V = 14 \text{m s}^{-1}$

Or using a vector diagram,
if the ball is kicked at 40°, then

$5t^2 = 6.1$

$\Rightarrow t = 1.10$ seconds

but $V = \dfrac{12}{t \cos 40°}$

$\Rightarrow V = 14 \text{m s}^{-1}$

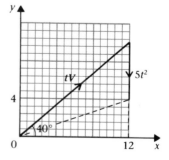

1.7 Modelling with projectiles

> What mathematical questions might you ask about juggling?

In order to discover more about the mathematics of juggling you will need to list as many questions as you can and sort out those you think you can tackle.

Some questions include:

- How high can a ball be thrown?
- How many balls can you throw in a minute (even if you cannot catch them)?
- Does the answer to one depend on the answer to the other?
- How far apart are the balls in the air?
- Can two people throwing to each other keep more balls in the air than two people juggling independently?
- What is the effect of air resistance?
- What effect does the shape of the ball have? Why do jugglers use clubs?

The last question will be too hard for you to answer now, but most of the earlier questions could be answered with a little experimentation and research.

2 Forces

2.1 Contact forces

> (a) What can be said about the four forces on the box if it does not move?
>
> (b) Draw a force diagram for the box above, replacing **N** and **F** by a single contact force **R**.

(a) If the box does not move then there is no change in momentum. The resultant force on the box is therefore zero. The normal contact force is balanced by the weight and the push is balanced by the friction force.

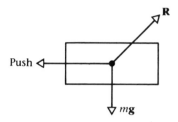

Describe each of the forces represented above. Draw another version of the force diagram replacing **R** by a normal contact force and a friction force.

There are three forces, the pull of the rope on the sledge, the weight of the sledge and the contact force between the slope and the sledge.

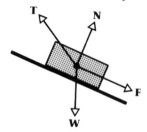

EXERCISE 1

1 (a) **A** is the normal contact force;
       B is the friction on the sledge;
       C is the weight of the sledge.

   (b) **D** is the lift force of air on the plane;
       E is the drag force of air resistance on the plane;
       F is the weight of the plane;
       G is the forward thrust of the jet (of air) on the plane due to the jet engines.

   (c) **H** is the normal contact force on the toy;
       I is its weight;
       J is the friction;
       K is the push of the child.

   (d) **L** is the tension force of the cable on the climber;
       M is the weight of the climber;
       O is the normal contact force of the ice face on the climber;
       N is the friction force of the ice face on the climber.

   (e) **P** is the friction force of the bat on the ball;
       Q is the weight of the ball;
       R is the normal contact force of the bat on the ball.

   (f) **S** is the upward lift force on the balloon carried by the hot air/cold air pressure differences;
       U is the force of the wind on the balloon;
       V is the weight of the balloon.

117

2

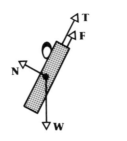

T is the tension in the rope;
F is the friction;
N is the normal contact force;
W is the weight.

3 (a)

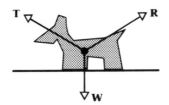

T is the tension in the rope;
R is the contact force;
W is the weight.

(b)

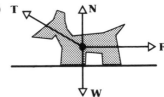

T is the tension in the rope;
N is the normal contact force.
W is the weight;
F is the friction force.

4 (a)

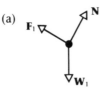

(b)

(c)

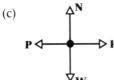

(d)

(e)

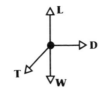

(f)

In the diagrams,

N is the normal contact force;
W is the weight;
P is push; R is contact force;
L is upthrust due to water;
D is the force due to air resistance or water;
F is the friction force;
F_1 is the friction force between the girl and the sledge;
F_2 is the friction force between the sledge and the ground;
T is tension.

(g)

2.2 Adding forces

How can you find the resultant of three or more forces?

For three forces **X**, **Y**, **Z** with resultant force **R**,
$$\mathbf{R} = \mathbf{X} + \mathbf{Y} + \mathbf{Z} = (\mathbf{X} + \mathbf{Y}) + \mathbf{Z} = \mathbf{X} + (\mathbf{Y} + \mathbf{Z}) = (\mathbf{X} + \mathbf{Z}) + \mathbf{Y}$$

This can be found by drawing the resultant of any pair of the vectors, then adding the resultant to the third vector. Alternatively the vectors can be drawn nose to tail to form a polygon. The resultant is the vector that joins the start of the vector chain to the finish.

For example:

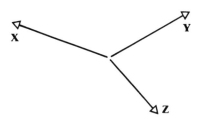
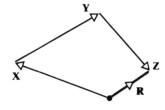

E X E R C I S E 2

1   (a) 6.4N at 39° to the force of 5N.

   (b) 1.3N, 88° above the force of 0.8N.

2   900N (898N to 3 s.f.,) at an angle of 13° or 14° (13.5° to 3 s.f.) to the force of 420N.

3   Between 112000 and 113000N in the direction of the ship.

4   215N at an angle of 22° to the vertical.

5   The angle between the forces is 117°. .

6   (a) **P** = 4.5N at an angle of 117° to the force of 2N.

   (b) **Q** = 11.7N at an angle of 149° to the force of 10N.

   (c) **F** = 5.4N at an angle of 112° to the force of 2N.

   (d) **T** = 4N at an angle of 120° to the force of 4N.

7   The force required = 98N.

   To estimate the least angle ϕ, first estimate the largest force the two people can apply, say $T = 200$N, then draw the triangle with sides 200, 200, 150, and measure the acute angle, which is 2ϕ.

   For $T = 200$, the angle is 22°. In general $\phi = \sin^{-1} \dfrac{75}{T}$.

2.3 Resolving forces

1 (a) $\begin{bmatrix} 43.3 \\ 25.0 \end{bmatrix}$

(b) The components are: 49.2 N up the slope; 8.68 N perpendicular to the slope.

(c) The components are 32.1 N down the slope; 38.3 N perpendicular to the slope.

2 (a)

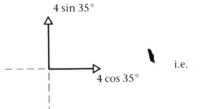

i.e.

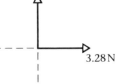

(b)

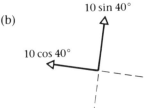

i.e.

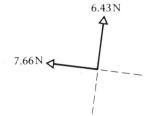

(c)

(d)

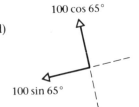

i.e

3 **(a)** **Force diagram** **Equivalent set of forces**

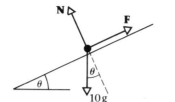 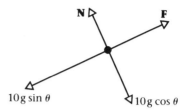

For equilibrium, the resultant force is zero.

i.e. $\begin{bmatrix} N - 10g \cos \theta \\ F - 10g \sin \theta \end{bmatrix} = \begin{bmatrix} 0 \\ 0 \end{bmatrix}$

Thus $F = 10g \sin \theta = 10g \sin 20° = 33.5$ newtons

(b) $F = 10g \sin \theta$ and $N = 10g \cos \theta$ newtons $\Rightarrow \dfrac{F}{N} = \tan \theta$

4 If you consider directions parallel to and perpendicular to the 11 newton force, then

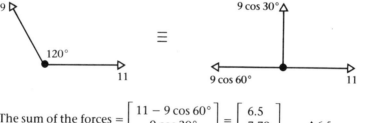

The sum of the forces $= \begin{bmatrix} 11 - 9 \cos 60° \\ 9 \cos 30° \end{bmatrix} = \begin{bmatrix} 6.5 \\ 7.79 \end{bmatrix}$

The resultant force $= \sqrt{(6.5^2 + 7.79^2)} = 10.1$ newtons

at an angle of $\tan^{-1} \left(\dfrac{6.5}{7.79} \right)$ or $39.8°$

The resultant is 10.1 newtons at an angle of approximately $40°$ with the 11 newton force.

5 **(a)** $\mathbf{R} = \begin{bmatrix} 2.60 \\ 1.50 \end{bmatrix} + \begin{bmatrix} -1.00 \\ 1.73 \end{bmatrix} + \begin{bmatrix} -1.97 \\ -0.347 \end{bmatrix} = \begin{bmatrix} -0.37 \\ 2.88 \end{bmatrix}$

This has magnitude 2.91 N, making an angle of $82.7°$ vertically up to the left.

(b) Take the x-axis parallel to the top right 2 N force.

$\mathbf{R} = \begin{bmatrix} 2 \\ 0 \end{bmatrix} + \begin{bmatrix} 1 \\ 1.73 \end{bmatrix} + \begin{bmatrix} -2 \\ 0 \end{bmatrix} + \begin{bmatrix} 1.29 \\ -1.53 \end{bmatrix}$

$= \begin{bmatrix} 0.29 \\ 0.20 \end{bmatrix}$

This has magnitude 0.35 N and cuts the $120°$ angle into $35°$ and $85°$.

121

6 $\mathbf{R} = \begin{bmatrix} 34.6 \\ 20 \end{bmatrix} + \begin{bmatrix} -35 \\ 0 \end{bmatrix} + \begin{bmatrix} 0 \\ -20 \end{bmatrix} = \begin{bmatrix} -0.4 \\ 0 \end{bmatrix}$

It will move in the direction of the force of 35 N.

7 Let the tensions be T_1 and T_2:

(a) $\begin{bmatrix} T_2 \sin 60 \\ T_2 \cos 60 \end{bmatrix} + \begin{bmatrix} -T_1 \sin 50 \\ T_1 \cos 50 \end{bmatrix} + \begin{bmatrix} 0 \\ -600 \end{bmatrix} = \begin{bmatrix} 0 \\ 0 \end{bmatrix}$

$\Rightarrow T_2 \sin 60 = T_1 \sin 50$
$\Rightarrow T_2 \cos 60 + T_1 \cos 50 = 600$
$\Rightarrow \dfrac{T_1 \sin 50}{\sin 60} \times \cos 60 + T_1 \cos 50 = 600$
$\Rightarrow T_1 = 553\,\text{N}$

and $T_2 = \dfrac{T_1 \sin 50}{60} = 489\,\text{N}$

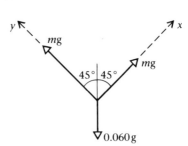

(b) Taking axes parallel and perpendicular to T_2;

$\begin{bmatrix} T_2 \\ 0 \end{bmatrix} + \begin{bmatrix} -T_1 \sin 20 \\ T_1 \cos 20 \end{bmatrix} + \begin{bmatrix} -600 \sin 30 \\ -600 \cos 30 \end{bmatrix} = \begin{bmatrix} 0 \\ 0 \end{bmatrix}$

$\Rightarrow T_2 - T_1 \sin 20 - 600 \sin 30 = 0$
and $T_1 \cos 20 - 600 \cos 30 = 0$
$\Rightarrow T_1 = \dfrac{600 \cos 30}{\cos 20} = 553\,\text{N}$

$T_2 = T_1 \sin 20 + 600 \sin 30 = 489\,\text{N}$

8 Taking axes as shown, by Newton's second law

$\begin{bmatrix} mg \\ 0 \end{bmatrix} + \begin{bmatrix} 0 \\ mg \end{bmatrix} = \begin{bmatrix} 0.060g \cos 45 \\ 0.060g \sin 45 \end{bmatrix}$

$\Rightarrow mg = \dfrac{0.060g}{\sqrt 2}$

so $m = \dfrac{3\sqrt 2}{100}\,\text{kg}$

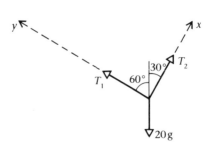

9 Let the tensions in the strings be T_1 and T_2 as shown.

By Newton's second law

$\begin{bmatrix} T_2 \\ 0 \end{bmatrix} + \begin{bmatrix} 0 \\ T_1 \end{bmatrix} = \begin{bmatrix} 200 \cos 30 \\ 200 \sin 30 \end{bmatrix}$

$T_2 = 100\sqrt 3$ newtons
$T_1 = 100$ newtons

2.4 Force and acceleration

EXERCISE 4

1 $N = 11.5\,\text{N}$

The acceleration of the block $a = \dfrac{15 \sin 40 - 2}{1.5}$

$$a = 5.1\,\text{m}\,\text{s}^{-2}$$

2 The acceleration of the trolley is $0.58\,\text{m}\,\text{s}^{-2}$.

3 The resultant force **R** $= 650 - 540 = 110\,\text{N}$ downwards, giving an acceleration of $1.7\,\text{m}\,\text{s}^{-2}$.

If the rope breaks, she will start to accelerate at $g = 10\,\text{m}\,\text{s}^{-2}$.

4 By Newton's second law, with air resistance R,

$$mg - R = ma$$
$$10 - R = 6 \;\Rightarrow\; R = 4$$

The air resistance is 4 newtons.

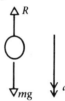

5 (a) If the woman is travelling with constant speed, she is in equilibrium so the contact force between her and the lift is 900 newtons.

(b) If she moves upward with acceleration $1.5\,\text{m}\,\text{s}^{-2}$ then if the normal contact force is R:

$$R - 900 = 90 \times 1.5$$
$$R = 1035 \text{ newtons}$$

(c) If she moves downward with acceleration $1.5\,\text{m}\,\text{s}^{-2}$ then if the normal contact force is R

$$900 - R = 90 \times 1.5$$
$$R = 755 \text{ newtons}$$

2.5 Models of static friction

> Are the models valid for the same range of N? Why is the inequality sign used?

The models are valid for different ranges of N. The first model applies to the data for small N. The second applies for large N. The third is an attempt to fit a curve that would be valid for most N. The inequality is used because friction can take any value up to the limiting value depending on the force being applied to it.

EXERCISE 5

1

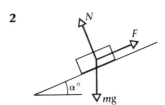

(a) Let F be the friction force and N the normal contact force. The crate is in equilibrium, so by Newton's second law,
$$F = 100 \sin 30° = 50 \text{ newtons}$$
and $N = 100 \cos 30° = 86.6 \text{ newtons}$

(b) But the crate is about to slip so $F = \mu N$
$$\Rightarrow 50 = 86.6\mu$$
$$\Rightarrow \mu = 0.577 \text{ to 3 s.f.}$$

2

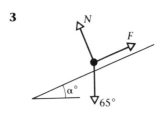

The rubber is on the point of slipping so $F = 0.7N$. But by Newton's second law along and perpendicular to the slope,

$$F = mg \sin \alpha \text{ and } N = mg \cos \alpha$$
so $\tan \alpha = 0.7$
$$\alpha = 35°$$
The table can be tilted to $35°$.

3

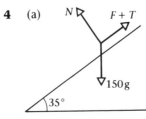

(a) Assume the climber is a particle and the friction between the slope and climber is F and $F \leqslant \mu N$.

By Newton's second law, $F = 650 \sin \alpha$ and $N = 650 \cos \alpha$. But the climber is on the point of slipping so $F = \mu N$.

$$650 \cos \alpha \times \mu = 650 \sin \alpha$$
$$\Rightarrow \mu = \tan \alpha$$
but $\mu = 1.2 \Rightarrow \alpha = 50.2$
So the greatest angle of slope is $50.2°$.

(b) The friction force is $650 \sin \alpha$
$$= 499 \text{ newtons}$$

4 (a)

If the sledge is about to slide down the slope the friction force acts up the slope and $F = \mu N$.

By Newton's second law,
$N = 1500 \cos 35 = 1229 \text{ newtons}$
and $F + T = 1500 \sin 35 = 860 \text{ newtons}$
but $F = 0.02N = 24.6 \text{ newtons}$
so $T = 835 \text{ newtons to 3 s.f.}$

(b)

If the sledge is about to slide up the slope the friction force F acts down the slope and $F = \mu N$.

By Newton's second law, $T - F = 860$ but F is still limiting so $F = 24.6$ newtons.

$$\Rightarrow T = 885 \text{ newtons to 3 s.f.}$$

5

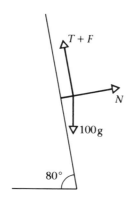

The climber is in equilibrium so $F \leq \mu N$.

$N = 1000 \cos 80 = 173.6$ newtons

and $T + F = 1000 \sin 80 = 984.8$ newtons.

Now $F \leq 0.9N = 156.2$

but F can act either up or down the slope depending on which way the body is trying to move, so

$$1141 \geq T \geq 828.6$$

The tension in the rope lies between 828.6 newtons and 1141 newtons.

2.6 Models of sliding friction

> What assumptions could you make about the magnitude and direction of the friction force in each of the situations above?

Different assumptions about friction may be reasonable in different situations; it may be reasonable to ignore friction on a puck sliding into goal, but the friction on an ice-skater cannot be ignored. (How can the skater change direction without friction?)

Looking at the pictures, you can see situations where it is important to increase friction (for example, by using big tyres or by placing the engine over the drive wheels) or to decrease friction (for example, by oozing slime or oiling an engine). Note that the slime has two roles. It can decrease friction, but it can also increase adhesion when the snail is climbing a slope. Good assumptions to make about friction include the following:

- Friction may increase to oppose sliding, up to some limit.

- At this limit, sliding or slipping/skidding may occur.

- The limit depends on the nature of the contact surface (for example, whether oiled or not) and on the normal contact force.

E X E R C I S E 6

1

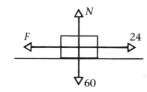

Let μ be the coefficient of sliding friction between the block and table.

The block is in equilibrium so by Newton's second law

$$F = 24 \text{ and } N = 60$$

But the block is sliding so $F = \mu N$

$$\Rightarrow 24 = 60\mu$$
$$\mu = 0.4$$

2

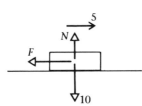

The puck is sliding freely so $F = 0.02N$

$$\Rightarrow F = 0.02$$

By Newton's second law $-F = ma$

$$\Rightarrow -0.02 = 0.1a$$
$$a = -0.2$$

but the initial speed is $10\,\mathrm{m\,s^{-1}}$
so $v = 10 - 0.2t \qquad t = 20$
$v = 6\,\mathrm{m\,s^{-1}}$ after 20 seconds

3

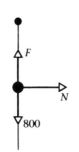

$F = 0.3N = 3$ newtons,
but by Newton's second law

$$0 - F = ma \qquad a = -3$$

Initial speed is $5\,\mathrm{m\,s^{-1}}$ so $v = 5 - 3t$
so when $v = 0, \quad t = \frac{5}{3}$

Now $s = ut + \frac{1}{2}at^2$
$$= 5 \times \frac{5}{3} + \frac{1}{2} \times -3 \times \frac{25}{9}$$
$$= \frac{25}{6} \text{ metres.}$$

4

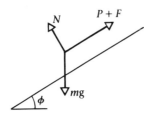

The normal contact force N must be horizontal.

Let all the mass of the gymnast be taken by his hands.

The gymnast is in equilibrium.

$$\Rightarrow F = 800$$

but $F = \mu N \Rightarrow N = \dfrac{800}{0.3}$

so $N = \dfrac{8000}{3}$ newtons

5E

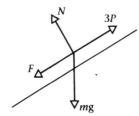

If the particle is sliding down the slope, F acts up the slope.

$P + F = mg \sin \phi$ and $N = mg \cos \phi$ by Newton's second law

but $F = \mu N$

so $P + \mu mg \cos \phi = mg \sin \phi$
$P = mg (\sin \phi - \mu \cos \phi)$

If the particle is sliding up the slope at constant speed F acts down the plane,

so $3P - F = mg \sin \phi$ and $N = mg \cos \phi$

$$\Rightarrow 3P = mg (\sin \phi + \mu \cos \phi)$$

but $P = mg (\sin \phi - \mu \cos \phi)$

$$\Rightarrow 3(\sin \phi - \mu \cos \phi) = \sin \phi + \mu \cos \phi$$
$$\Rightarrow 2 \sin \phi = 4\mu \cos \phi$$
$$\tan \phi = 2\mu$$

3 Acceleration and circular motion

3.1 The motion of the Moon

1 (a) Gravitational force $= \dfrac{GMm}{r^2} = \dfrac{6.67 \times 10^{-11} \times 7.34 \times 10^{22} \times 5.98 \times 10^{24}}{(3.8 \times 10^8)^2}$ N

$$= 2.0 \times 10^{20}\,\text{N (to 2 s.f.)}$$

(b) The acceleration of the Moon is $\dfrac{2.03 \times 10^{20}}{7.34 \times 10^{22}}\,\text{m s}^{-2}$

$$= 2.8 \times 10^{-3}\,\text{m s}^{-2}\ \text{(to 2 s.f.)}$$

It acts towards the centre of the Earth.

2 (a) Using $R = \dfrac{GMm}{r^2}$, $\quad R = \dfrac{2 \times 10^{30} \times 5.98 \times 10^{24} \times 6.67 \times 10^{-11}}{1.50^2 \times 10^{22}}$

$$= 3.55 \times 10^{22}\,\text{newtons}$$

The acceleration is $5.93 \times 10^{-3}\,\text{m s}^{-2}$ towards the Sun.

(b) If $r = 1.52 \times 10^{11}$, $\quad \dfrac{R_1}{R} = \dfrac{1.5^2}{1.52^2} \Rightarrow R_1 = 0.974R$

$$= 3.46 \times 10^{22}\,\text{newtons}$$

If $r = 1.47 \times 10^{11}$, $\quad R_2 = 3.70 \times 10^{22}$ newtons
The range is from 3.46×10^{22} to 3.70×10^{22} newtons.

3 Assume Skylab is a particle of mass $90\,600$ kg, a distance $(434 + 6378)$ km above the Earth's centre.

Using Newton's law of gravitation

$$R = \dfrac{GMm}{r^2} = \dfrac{6.67 \times 10^{-11} \times 9.06 \times 10^4 \times 5.98 \times 10^{24}}{6.812^2 \times 10^{12}}$$

The force of attraction is 7.79×10^5 newtons.

3.2 Angular speed and velocity

> (a) Calculate the position vector **r** and the velocity vector **v** for time t where t = 0.5, 1, 1.5, 2, 2.5 and 3 seconds.
>
> (b) On a sheet of graph paper, draw a circle (reduced scale) to represent the penny on the turntable and mark the position and velocity vectors calculated above.
>
> What can you say about the magnitude and direction of the velocity vector?
>
> What can you say about the acceleration, $\dfrac{d\mathbf{v}}{dt}$, of the penny?

(a)

t	0.5	1	1.5	2	2.5	3
r	$\begin{bmatrix} 0.054 \\ 0.084 \end{bmatrix}$	$\begin{bmatrix} -0.042 \\ 0.091 \end{bmatrix}$	$\begin{bmatrix} -0.099 \\ 0.014 \end{bmatrix}$	$\begin{bmatrix} -0.065 \\ -0.076 \end{bmatrix}$	$\begin{bmatrix} 0.028 \\ -0.096 \end{bmatrix}$	$\begin{bmatrix} 0.096 \\ -0.028 \end{bmatrix}$
v	$\begin{bmatrix} -0.17 \\ 0.11 \end{bmatrix}$	$\begin{bmatrix} -0.18 \\ -0.08 \end{bmatrix}$	$\begin{bmatrix} -0.03 \\ -0.20 \end{bmatrix}$	$\begin{bmatrix} 0.15 \\ -0.13 \end{bmatrix}$	$\begin{bmatrix} 0.19 \\ 0.06 \end{bmatrix}$	$\begin{bmatrix} 0.06 \\ 0.19 \end{bmatrix}$

(b) The velocity is of constant magnitude. The direction is always perpendicular to the radius. The acceleration is of constant magnitude. The direction is always towards the centre.

EXERCISE 2

1 50 r.p.m. $= \dfrac{50 \times 2\pi}{60}$ rad s^{-1}

Speed of tip is $\dfrac{4 \times 50 \times 2\pi}{60}$ m s^{-1} = 21 m s^{-1} (to 2 s.f.)

2 Angular speed, $\omega = \dfrac{v}{r} = \dfrac{1}{0.1}$ rad s^{-1} = 10 rad s^{-1}

3 500 r.p.m. $= \dfrac{500 \times 2\pi}{60}$ rad s$^{-1} \approx 52$ rad s^{-1}

1000 r.p.m. ≈ 105 rad s^{-1}

The speed of a point on the drum varies between $\dfrac{500 \times 2\pi \times 0.6}{60}$ m s^{-1}

and double this, i.e. between 31.4 and 63 m s^{-1}.

4 (a) $v = r\omega = \dfrac{6.37 \times 10^6 \times 2\pi}{24 \times 60 \times 60}\,\mathrm{m\,s^{-1}} \approx 464\,\mathrm{m\,s^{-1}}$

(b) Speed at the north pole is zero.

5 (a) Angular speed $= 3\,\mathrm{rad\,s^{-1}}$

$\qquad\qquad\qquad\qquad\qquad = 3 \div 2\pi$ revolutions per second

$\qquad$ Time for 1 revolution $= \dfrac{2\pi}{3}$ seconds

(b) Angular speed $= \omega\,\mathrm{rad\,s^{-1}}$

$\qquad\qquad\qquad\qquad\qquad = \dfrac{\omega}{2\pi}$ revolutions per second

$\qquad$ Time for 1 revolution $= T = \dfrac{2\pi}{\omega}$

6E The cotton on the outside of the reel unwinds at $3\,\mathrm{m\,s^{-1}}$.

The angular speed is $\dfrac{3}{0.02} = 150\,\mathrm{rad\,s^{-1}}$.

When the reel is nearly empty the angular speed is
$\dfrac{3}{0.01}\,\mathrm{rad\,s^{-1}} = 300\,\mathrm{rad\,s^{-1}}$.

After 25 minutes half the cotton will have gone, but the diameter of the reel will be greater than $1.5\,\mathrm{cm}$, so the angular speed is less than $200\,\mathrm{rad\,s^{-1}}$.

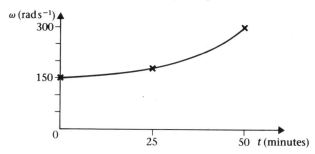

3.3 Circular motion

(a) Find the velocity by differentiation and show that its magnitude is constant. What is its direction?

(b) Show that the acceleration can be written as

$$a = r\omega^2 \begin{bmatrix} -\cos \omega t \\ -\sin \omega t \end{bmatrix} \qquad \text{or} \qquad a = -\omega^2 \mathbf{r}$$

What is its direction?

Show that its magnitude is $a = r\omega^2 = \dfrac{v^2}{r}$.

(a) $\mathbf{v} = \begin{bmatrix} -r\omega \sin \omega t \\ r\omega \cos \omega t \end{bmatrix}$

$v = \sqrt{(r^2\omega^2 \sin^2 \omega t + r^2\omega^2 \cos^2 \omega t)} = r\omega$

The direction of the radius is $\begin{bmatrix} -\cos \omega t \\ -\sin \omega t \end{bmatrix}$

so the direction of the velocity is perpendicular to the radius.

(b) $\mathbf{v} = \begin{bmatrix} -r\omega \sin \omega t \\ r\omega \cos \omega t \end{bmatrix} \Rightarrow \mathbf{a} = \begin{bmatrix} -r\omega^2 \cos \omega t \\ -r\omega^2 \sin \omega t \end{bmatrix} = -\omega^2 \mathbf{r}$

so $a = \omega^2 r = r\left(\dfrac{v}{r}\right)^2 = \dfrac{v^2}{r}$

The direction is towards the centre of the circle.

> When seen on television an astronaut seems to float effortlessly round the capsule. Does this mean that the astronaut is weightless?

No! The astronaut has the same acceleration towards the centre of the Earth as does the capsule. The astronaut's weight is the force of gravitation that causes the acceleration. Without it he would head off into deep space at a constant velocity.

The appearance of weightlessness is due to the fact that there is no contact force between the astronaut and the capsule because they are both moving freely with the same acceleration. It is, nevertheless, wrong to refer to the astronaut as being weightless.

EXERCISE 3

1 (a) One revolution in 27.32 days is $\dfrac{2\pi}{27.32 \times 24 \times 3600}$ rad s^{-1}

$\approx 2.7 \times 10^{-6}$ rad s^{-1}

(b) Acceleration $= \dfrac{3.8 \times 10^8 \times (2\pi)^2}{(27.32 \times 24 \times 3600)^2}$ m s^{-2}

$\approx 2.7 \times 10^{-3}$ m s^{-2}

(c) Allowing for inaccuracy of data, the answers are the same.

2   120 km h^{-1} = $\dfrac{120 \times 1000}{3600}$ m s^{-1}

The acceleration $\dfrac{v^2}{r} = 30$ m s^{-2},

so the radius is $\left(\dfrac{120}{3.6}\right)^2 \div 30$ m ≈ 37 metres

3 $10 \text{r.p.m.} = \dfrac{10 \times 2\pi}{60} \text{rad s}^{-1} = \dfrac{\pi}{3} = 1.05 \text{rad s}^{-1}$

(a) Her speed is $1 \times 1.05 \text{m s}^{-1} \approx 1 \text{m s}^{-1}$

Her acceleration is $1 \times \left(\dfrac{\pi}{3}\right)^2 \approx 1.1 \text{m s}^{-2}$

(b) Her speed is 2.1m s^{-1} and her acceleration is 2.2m s^{-2} (to 2 s.f.).

At 1 metre from the centre, the force towards the centre is $30 \times 1.1 \text{N}$ or 33 N.

At 2 metres from the centre the force is doubled to 66 N.

4

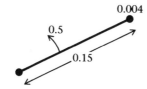

The acceleration is $0.5^2 \times 0.15 = 0.0375 \text{m s}^{-2}$ towards the centre of the circle.

$F = 0.004 \times 0.0375 = 0.00015 \text{N}$

This force is towards the centre of the turntable and is due to friction.

$\dfrac{F}{N} \leqslant \mu \Rightarrow \dfrac{0.00015}{0.04} \leqslant \mu$

$\Rightarrow \mu \geqslant 0.00375$

The coefficient of friction is greater than or equal to 0.003 75.

5

Let the block have mass m kilograms and be modelled as a particle 0.2 metres from the axis of rotation. Let the angular speed be $\omega \text{rad s}^{-1}$.

Acceleration $= \omega^2 \times 0.2$ towards centre, force $= 0.2\,m\omega^2$

In limiting friction $F = \mu N = 0.3\,mg$

$0.2 m\omega^2 = 0.3 mg \Rightarrow \omega = 3.87 \text{rad s}^{-1}$ (to 3 s.f.)

The turntable must spin with an angular speed of over 3.87rad s^{-1} for the block to slide off.

6E

Problem

1 revolution in 6 seconds $= \dfrac{2\pi}{6} \text{rad s}^{-1}$

$= 1.05 \text{rad s}^{-1}$

Set up a model	Assume each skater is 0.8 metre from elbow to elbow. You can model the skater as a particle half way along this 80 cm length. Assume that the mass of each skater is 65 kg.

| Analyse the problem | The furthest skater makes a circle of radius 3.6 metres and the central skaters make circles of radius 0.4 metres. |

The speeds of the outside skaters are therefore $3.8\,\mathrm{m\,s^{-1}}$ and those of the central skaters are $0.42\,\mathrm{m\,s^{-1}}$.

| Interpret /validate | The acceleration of the outside pair is $3.96\,\mathrm{m\,s^{-2}}$ radially inwards. Now $\mathbf{F} = m\mathbf{a}$ so the force is 257 newtons to 3 s.f. (Remember this is the resultant force. What do you think the force on each arm of the central skaters will be?) |

3.4 Acceleration

> How have the magnitudes of the accelerations at P and R been calculated? Why is no acceleration shown at Q?

The acceleration is zero on the straight sections as both the speed and direction are constant. On the bends the speed is still constant but the direction changes so the acceleration is $\dfrac{v^2}{r}$.

Where $r = 0.3\,\mathrm{m}$ the acceleration is about $13\,\mathrm{m\,s^{-2}}$.
Where $r = 0.5\,\mathrm{m}$ the acceleration is about $8\,\mathrm{m\,s^{-2}}$.

The tighter the bend the greater the acceleration at any given speed.

E X E R C I S E   4

1   (a)

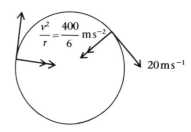

(b) The velocity is not constant since its direction is changing as the skater moves round the circle.

(c) The acceleration has constant magnitude but its direction changes as the skater moves round the circle. It is always perpendicular to the velocity.

2

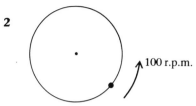

$$100 \text{ r.p.m} = \frac{100 \times 2\pi}{60} \text{rad s}^{-1}$$

$$= 10\frac{\pi}{3} \text{ rad s}^{-1}$$

The radius is $\frac{27}{2}$ cm or $\frac{0.27}{2}$ m.

The acceleration of the object is $r\omega^2 = \frac{0.27}{2} \times \left(10\frac{\pi}{3}\right)^2 = 15 \text{ m s}^{-2}$ directed towards the centre of the drum.

Using Newton's second law, $F = ma$

$$|F| = 0.2 \times 15 = 3$$

The resultant force is 3 newtons towards the centre of the circle.

3 (a)

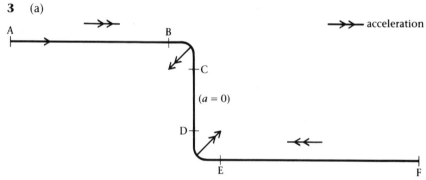

(b) Rate of change of speed:

AB : rate of change of speed = |acceleration|
BC : rate of change of speed = 0
CD : rate of change of speed = 0
DE : rate of change of speed = 0
EF : rate of change of speed = −|acceleration|

4

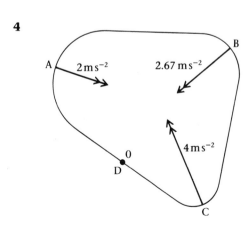

5E (a) $\mathbf{v} = \begin{bmatrix} 2t \times -10\sin t^2 \\ 2t \times 10\cos t^2 \end{bmatrix} = 20\begin{bmatrix} -t\sin t^2 \\ t\cos t^2 \end{bmatrix} = 20t\begin{bmatrix} -\sin t^2 \\ \cos t^2 \end{bmatrix}$

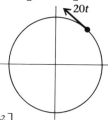

The velocity has magnitude 20*t*, and is a **variable**. In fact, the speed is increasing and the motion is **not** uniform.

The direction of the velocity $\begin{bmatrix} -\sin t^2 \\ \cos t^2 \end{bmatrix}$ is still tangential to the circle.

$$\mathbf{a} = 20\begin{bmatrix} -\sin t^2 - 2t^2\cos t^2 \\ \cos t^2 - 2t^2\sin t^2 \end{bmatrix}$$

$$= 20\begin{bmatrix} -\sin t^2 \\ \cos t^2 \end{bmatrix} - 40t^2\begin{bmatrix} \cos t^2 \\ \sin t^2 \end{bmatrix}$$

(b) The acceleration has two parts, $20\begin{bmatrix} -\sin t^2 \\ \cos t^2 \end{bmatrix}$ and $-40\,t^2\begin{bmatrix} \cos t^2 \\ \sin t^2 \end{bmatrix}$

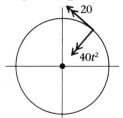

The first part has magnitude $20\,\mathrm{m\,s^{-2}}$ and is tangential. The second part has magnitude $40t^2\,\mathrm{m\,s^{-2}}$ and is towards the centre of the circle.

(c) The acceleration is **in general** not towards the centre of the circle. There is often, as in this case, a tangential component. If the angular speed is constant (the speed is constant), then the tangential component is zero and the acceleration **is** directed towards the centre. This special case is called uniform circular motion and has been the subject of this chapter.

4 Rigid bodies

4.2 Moments

> Why is the moment of the force **R** about the pivot equal to zero?

The distance of **R** from the hinge is zero so its moment about the hinge is

$$R \times 0 = 0$$

If the moments are taken about a point A, any force through A will have zero moment.

EXERCISE 1

1 Total moment about A = $50 \times 4 + 100 \times 6$
$$= 800 \,\text{Nm anticlockwise}$$

2 The moment of **P** about O is $5 \times 6 = 30 \,\text{Nm}$ clockwise.
The moment of **Q** about O is $8 \times \sin 30° \times 7 = 28 \,\text{Nm}$ anticlockwise.
The moment of **R** about O is zero.

3 The moment of the force **W** about O is $Wa \sin \phi \,\text{Nm}$ clockwise.
The moment of the force **P** about O is $2Pa \cos \phi \,\text{Nm}$ anticlockwise.

4 (a) The moment of the 10 newton force about O = $10 \times 0.24 \times \sin 50°$
$$= 1.84 \,\text{Nm clockwise.}$$
The moment of the 6 newton force about O = $6 \times 0.40 \times \sin 50°$
$$= 1.84 \,\text{Nm anticlockwise.}$$
The moment of the 16 newton force about O = 16×0
$$= 0$$

(b) The moment of the 10 newton force about A = 10×0
$$= 0$$
The moment of the 6 newton force about A = $6 \times 0.64 \times \sin 50°$
$$= 2.94 \,\text{Nm anticlockwise.}$$
The moment of the 16 newton force about A = $16 \times 0.24 \times \sin 50°$
$$= 2.94 \,\text{Nm clockwise.}$$

5 The moment of the force **T** about O = $Tl \sin \phi$ but $\sin \phi$ is a maximum when $\phi = 90°$, so the turning effect will be greatest when $\sin \phi = 1$. She should pull vertically upwards.

6 The wheel of the wheelbarrow acts as a pivot. If the wheelbarrow handles are three times as far from the wheel as the skip is, then Carole's lifting force is approximately 300 N.

7E The line of action of Winston's weight
will be $2 \cos 30° + 2 \sin 30°$ metres from
the pivot, so Winston's weight will
produce a clockwise moment of
$$200 (2 \cos 30° + 2 \sin 30°) = 546 \,\text{Nm}$$
Josie's weight will be $2 \cos 30° - 2 \sin 30°$
metres from the pivot and will
produce an anticlockwise moment of
$$600 (2 \cos 30° - 2 \sin 30°) = 439 \,\text{Nm}$$
Winston's weight has the greater turning
effect.

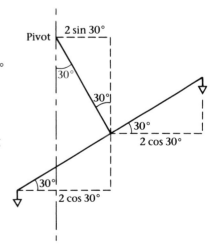

8E (a) Assume the plank is weightless and that Josie is x metres from the pivot. The moment of Josie about the pivot = $600x$ anticlockwise. The moment of Winston is $200(3-x)$ clockwise. These must balance, so $600x = 600 - 200x \Rightarrow x = 0.75$

Josie must be 0.75 metres from the pivot.

(b) The plank would provide an extra clockwise moment and the pivot would therefore be slightly further away from Josie than the 0.75 metres calculated in part (a).

4.3 Equilibrium

EXERCISE 2

1 The mass of the ruler acts through its midpoint, the point of support. For equilibrium, the total moment about the support is zero.

The force due to the m_1 gram mass is $0.001\,m_1\,$g downwards. That due to the m_2 mass is $0.001m_2$g.

Taking moments about the support

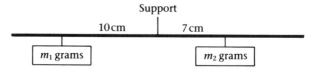

For equilibrium, $0.001m_1$g $\times 0.1 - 0.001m_2$g $\times 0.07 = 0$
so $m_1 = 0.7m_2$, when $m_1 = 49$, $m_2 = 70$
The second mass is 70 grams.

2 Taking moments about A the body is in equilibrium so the sum of the moments is zero.

$$T \times 2a = Wa \cos \theta$$
$$\text{so } T = 0.5W \cos \theta$$

3 If the string makes an angle of 60° then $T \times 2a \sin 60 = Wa \cos \theta$ so $T = 0.577W \cos \theta$, which is greater than before.

4 (a) The moments of the component about the origin are 3×2 clockwise and 4×5 anticlockwise
The sum $= -6 + 20 = 14\,$Nm anticlockwise

(b) The resultant force is 5 newtons in the direction shown.

Its moment about the origin $= 5 \times ON$

But $ON = 3.5 \sin \phi$ where $\sin \phi = 0.8$

$ON = 2.8$

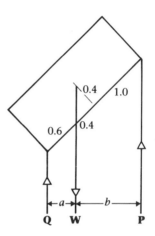

The moment of the resultant force about the origin is $5 \times 2.8 = 14\,Nm$ anticlockwise.

5 Assuming the weight is equally distributed over the box (and its interior) – which is not very likely – the diagram represents the situation:

From the diagram

$a = 0.6 \cos 45°$
$b = 1.4 \cos 45°$

Taking moments about the bottom corner

$a \times 750 = (a + b)P$
$\Rightarrow P = 225$ newtons

Resolving vertically, $P + Q = 750 \Rightarrow Q = 525$ newtons

The strongest man needs to be at the bottom. (However, the top position is the most difficult and uncomfortable in practice.)

Each hand should provide half the required lift so the supporting force provided by each hand is 262.5 newtons from the man at the bottom and 112.5 newtons from the man at the top.

6 (a)

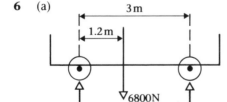

Assume the load on each of the front wheels is the same.
Assume that the load on each of the rear wheels is the same.
Assume that the contact force between the wheels and the road is normal to the road surface.

Taking moments about the rear axle,
$3 \times F = 1.2 \times 6800 \Rightarrow F = 2720$ newtons
$R + F = 6800$ newtons, so $R = 4080$ newtons

The total reaction at each front wheel is 1360 newtons.

The total reaction at each rear wheel is 2040 newtons.

(b) With the extra 600N of luggage, making a total weight of 7400N, the force at each wheel is multiplied by $\frac{7400}{6800}$. Each rear wheel carries 2220N and each front wheel carries 1480N.

(c) With the luggage in the boot the forces acting are as shown:

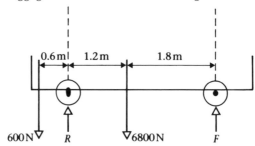

Considering moments about the front axle:

$$R \times 3 = 600 \times 3.6 + 6800 \times 1.8 \Rightarrow R = 4800 \text{ newtons}$$

Considering moments about the rear axle:

$$F \times 3 + 600 \times 0.6 = 6800 \times 1.2 \Rightarrow F = 2600 \text{ newtons}$$

Each rear wheel will carry 2400 newtons.
Each front wheel will carry 1300 newtons.

7E

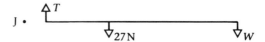

With the notation in the figure:
Taking moments about J: $T \times 0.02 = 27 \times 0.13 + W \times 0.3$

(a) When $W = 0$, $T = 175.5$
The tension is about 180 newtons.

(b) When $W = 45$, $T = 850.5$
The tension is about 850 newtons.

This is, of course, a very greatly simplified model of the real situation.

4.4 Centre of gravity

E X E R C I S E 3

1 (a) Taking moments about the centre of the 3 N weight, C, as the pivot
$2 \times 0.4 + 2 \times 0.8 = 7X$ where X is the distance of the centre of gravity from C.
$X = 0.343$ metres.
The centre of gravity is 34.3 cm from the 3 newton weight (to 3 s.f.).

(b) Taking moments about the unweighted end of the rod, A,
$0.5 \times 2 + 1 \times 3 = 5X$
$X = 0.8$ metres.
The centre of gravity is 80 cm from the unweighted end of the rod.

2

| Movement | Displacement in the direction of the | | |
	x-axis	y-axis	z-axis
(i)	zero	zero	positive
(ii)	zero	positive	negative
(iii)	positive	negative	zero
(iv)	positive	zero	negative

4.5 Centre of mass

EXERCISE 4

1 Assume that the centres of gravity of the spheres are at their geometric centres. The total mass of the toy is 100 grams.

Taking the axes shown, if the centre of gravity of the toy is at $(\bar{x}, \bar{y})$

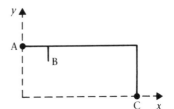

taking moments about A, $1 \times \bar{x} = 0.2 \times 60$
$$\Rightarrow \quad \bar{x} = 12$$

Similarly $\bar{y} = 20$

Hence the pin must be fixed a distance 12 cm along the rod from the centre of the large sphere and must be 5 cm long.

2 (a)

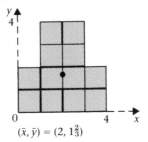

$(\bar{x}, \bar{y}) = (2, 1\frac{2}{3})$

(b)

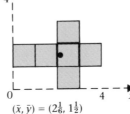

$(\bar{x}, \bar{y}) = (2\frac{1}{6}, 1\frac{1}{2})$

(c)

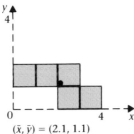

$(\bar{x}, \bar{y}) = (2.1, 1.1)$

(d)

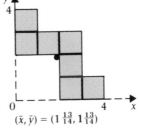

$(\bar{x}, \bar{y}) = (1\frac{13}{14}, 1\frac{13}{14})$

3 The Earth and Moon can be replaced by point masses of 5.98×10^{24} kg and 7.34×10^{22} kg, a distance of 384 000 km apart (average value). Their joint centre of mass therefore lies 4660 km from the Earth's centre (to 3 s.f.), approximately 1700 km below the Earth's surface.

5 Extended investigations

5.2 Getting started

By using simple apparatus, by going to look at a slide or by simply sitting and thinking, write down anything that needs to be taken into account if you have the task of designing a children's slide.

Compare your list with the samples of students' work given in the solutions.

Design a slide
ideas
safety, materials, age of children, steepness of slide
height of top from ground, desired top speed,
maximum speed on leaving slide.

General Criteria

Smooth surfaces to limit friction.
Steep enough to slide.
Must level off at the bottom so they can
stop before the slide ends.
Sides so that they don't fall off – smooth
Strong
Weatherproof
Walled in at top.
Wide enough
Bend in bottom suitably shaped.

General ideas

To obtain enough speed, the slide must be steep enough, smooth enough and long enough.

For safety the slide must have restrictions on the sides, a run off at the end, must not be too high.

design features are: wide enough, strong enough, attractive colour and texture.

Identify those problems that you think you can solve or model by using Newtonian mechanics.

Compare your list with those in the solutions.

Some problems which I could solve are

Where is the child on the slide going fastest?
How long a horizontal bit of slide will be needed to slow them down to a stop?
How steep does the angled bit of slide need to be so the children slide?
What coefficient of friction is likely?
How long will the ride down the slide take?

Mathematical problems
1. coeff of friction between different materials and the surface of the slide
2. Weight/mass of person may have to be known for slowing distances on runway, speed on slope, velocity at the bottom.
3. Angle of elevation of slope, length of slope, height of slope, length of runway

How long should the slide be
(a) its slope (b) its horizontal part?
What angle should it make?
What effect does the weight of
the child have?
What clothes should they wear?
What curve should I have at
the bottom?
Must they stop before they reach
the end of the slide?

In the list above, the problem 'What curve should it make at the bottom?' was too difficult for the student to solve. She overcame this by modelling the slide as two straight sections with no change in speed between the two.

Some examples of problems rejected by the students because they could not be solved by Newtonian mechanics were

- How wide should the slide be to fit 5–8 year olds?

- What is a reasonable width of step on the stairs?

- What colour do children favour for a slide?

- What materials are most robust?